Fire Them Up!

Fire Them Up!

7 Simple Secrets to:

- Inspire Colleagues, Customers, and Clients
- Sell Yourself, Your Vision, and Your Values
- Communicate with Charisma and Confidence

CARMINE GALLO

John Wiley & Sons, Inc.

Published by John Wiley & Sons, Inc., Hoboken, New Jersey.
Published simultaneously in Canada.

Wiley Bicentennial Logo: Richard J. Pacifico

For general information on our other products and services or for technical support, please contact our Customer Care Department within the United States at (800) 762-2974, outside the United States at (317) 572-3993 or fax (317) 572-4002.

Wiley also publishes its books in a variety of electronic formats. Some content that appears in print may not be available in electronic books. For more information about Wiley products, visit our Web site at www.wiley.com.

Library of Congress Cataloging-in-Publication Data:

Gallo, Carmine.
   Fire them up! : 7 simple secrets to inspire colleagues, customers, and Clients, sell yourself, your vision, and your values, communicate with Charisma and confidence / Carmine Gallo.
     p. cm.
   ISBN 978-0-470-16566-9 (cloth)
1. Business communication.   2. Communication in management.
3. Communication in organizations.   I. Title.
   HF5718.G353 2008
658.4′5–dc22   2007014932

Printed in the United States of America.

10 9 8 7 6 5 4 3 2 1

To Josephine and Lela. My girls, my inspiration.

Contents

Acknowledgments

I know it is customary to thank spouses at the end of the acknowledgments section, but this time my wife deserves much of the credit. Vanessa was instrumental in getting crucial material to the publisher on time. She spent countless hours retrieving the permissions required to include the interviews and photographs in this book. One cannot be blessed with a greater inspiration by their side. Thank you, Vanessa, for making my life richer than I could ever imagine.

Many thanks to my editor at John Wiley & Sons, Richard Narramore, for believing in the power of this content to make a difference in the lives of its readers. Richard's suggestions gave this book an entirely new dimension. Special praise for Wiley editorial assistant Tiffany Groglio. Her title doesn't do justice to her gifts. She is a consummate editor and unbelievably professional. Tiffany is nothing short of amazing. Everyone at Wiley is top notch, and my thanks go out to all involved in editing, design, marketing, publicity, and sales. Wiley does it right from start to finish.

My agent at New England Publishing Associates, Edward Knappman, continues to be one of my strongest supporters. His advice has always been spot on. Thank you, Ed.

Thank you to everyone who generously gave of their time to participate in this work. You are exceptional people who raise the bar for the rest of us: Jay Adelson, Cliff Atkinson, Ron Clark, Simon Cooper, Nancy Duarte, Doug Ducey, Peter Fleisher, Krista Hawkins, Wendy Kopp, Robert Labrenz, Wayne Leonard, Bob Levinson, Marissa Mayer, Mark Mastrov, Matt McCauley, Mike McCue,

Michelle Peluso, Bill Powanda, Jason Rhodes, Al Stubblefield, Richard Tait, and Jim Thompson.

Although the next individuals were not directly interviewed for this book, these authors have influenced and inspired me: Marcus Buckingham, Jim Collins, Stephen. R. Covey, Wayne W. Dyer, Chip Heath and Dan Heath, John Maxwell, and Tim Sanders. Thank you, gentlemen, for your insights and contribution to improving the way business is done.

One cannot be blessed with a more supportive family. Many thanks to my parents, Francesco and Giuseppina. Thanks also to Tino, Donna, Francesco, Nicholas, Ken, Patty, and my dear and close friends.

My girls, Josephine and Lela, are too young to read this today, but when they do, I want them to know that the joy on their faces has made this daddy proud. They make every day an inspiration.

PART I

The 7 Simple Secrets

INTRODUCTION

Our Chief Want

> Our chief want is someone who will inspire us to be what we know we could be.
>
> —Ralph Waldo Emerson

You have the power to inspire anyone, anywhere, anytime. You may not have a leadership title, but you exert influence over someone every day. Whether you are a Fortune 500 chief executive or the head of a household, you are in the motivational business. Regardless of your role, you play the part of chief inspiration officer for someone at work, at home, or in your community. The 7 Simple Secrets revealed in this book hold the key to successfully selling yourself, your vision, and your values to everyone within your sphere of influence. As you develop the astonishing communications skills shared by the world's most inspiring men and women, you will enjoy far more successful and fulfilling relationships with your colleagues, clients, employees, and anyone in your personal or professional life.

In order for these strategies to work, you need to see yourself as the leader of your personal brand. How you talk, walk, and look reflect on that brand, and you are in sole command of the impression you make. If you fail to connect, you will lose the admiration of the people you hope to influence. But once you master the 7 Simple Secrets, you will be known among your peers as an individual who speaks with confidence and charisma. A door will open to a new world of achievement because the stories you tell will have the power to inspire, motivate, and persuade. The verbal pictures you paint will be so vivid and bright that the rest of us will want to climb aboard for the ride. The language you use will be so positive and optimistic that your presence will energize us, making us feel better about ourselves and our roles in the world.

Whose "Secrets" Are These?

When conference organizers invite me to speak on the topic of business communications, they often introduce me as a "motivational speaker." While I am flattered and eager to share what I have learned, I quickly point out that if you have to hire a motivational speaker to fire up your people, you've already lost them. You are the one they turn to for motivation day after day, not me. I'm not the one who spends eight, nine, ten hours a day alongside them. You are the one who must develop your skills of persuasion to inspire those around you. In this book, you will learn from the best. The 7 Simple Secrets revealed belong to the men and women who, by the power of their words, deeds, and demeanor, inspire everyone around them. They include:

- Leaders who run companies such as The Ritz-Carlton, Google, Gymboree, Cold Stone Creamery, 24 Hour Fitness, Travelocity, Starbucks, and many other well-known brands.
- A company president who has built a culture so synonymous with extraordinary service that every year hundreds of business professionals pay thousands of dollars to learn his company's techniques.

- Managers who have transformed their companies from second-tier organizations into nationally ranked Best Places to Work.
- A Princeton graduate whose idealistic vision inspired thousands of college seniors to join her cause, landing her on the cover of *Fortune* magazine.
- An entrepreneur who created a worldwide brand sensation after sketching his idea on the back of a napkin and firing up the people around him to follow his vision.
- A teacher whose techniques are so effective that a television movie was based on his experiences.

These men and women come from different backgrounds, generations, and industries, but they share one quality in common: the ability to inspire others to higher levels of achievement and to win over others with the power of their words. Their insights will change the way you see yourself as a brand and how you communicate the vision behind your values. A world of potential exists in each and every one of us: a potential unleashed by those who speak the language of success. In the pages to follow, the language will be revealed.

The techniques are called "simple secrets" because they really are simple. All you have to do is adopt the model in your everyday communications: presentations, pitches, meetings, speeches, interviews, emails, Webcasts, blogs, or however you articulate your story to those you intend to influence. Most of the books, white papers, and research studies on the subject of business communications are long, confusing, and boring—the exact opposite of the skills you need to inspire. You will be pleased to know that I have studied the research to save you the hassle. I have also spent nearly twenty years as a communications professional: as a CNN business correspondent, television anchor, radio host, columnist, author, speaker, and communications coach who works with top executives at the world's most admired brands. My clients' brands touch your life each and every day. From your bank, to your computer, to the products you buy and the foods you eat, my clients make and sell the things that you can't live without. My job is to make sure that the leaders who run those companies craft and deliver messages that will electrify their audiences. Hundreds of business professionals, from CEOs to entrepreneurs, have gone from dull to dazzling using the model in this book. I get really pumped up about these principles because I see how they have changed the lives and careers of people who have mastered them.

The word "inspire" means to elicit fervent enthusiasm. In other words, to fire people up! Think about the roles you play in business and the opportunities you have to inspire, motivate, and persuade the people around you:

- *CEO.* Rallying your employees, customers, and investors to embrace your vision.
- *Salesperson.* Turning prospects into customers and customers into evangelists.
- *Manager.* Firing up employees about new products and the future of the company.
- *Merchant.* Encouraging your staff to exceed the expectations of your customers by offering mind-blowing service.
- *Entrepreneur.* Electrifying your investors, partners, employees, and customers about your new company and its potential to change the world.
- *Coach.* Motivating your team to play harder, learn from their mistakes, and celebrate their losses and victories with class.
- *Teacher.* Encouraging your students to learn discipline, study hard, and commit themselves to reaching their potential in school and in life.
- *Pastor.* Energizing your congregation to live their faith and values in the community after they leave their place of worship.
- *Parent.* Convincing your children to model your high ethical and moral standards.

These desired actions begin and end with how effectively you communicate the story behind your vision. Some people have an appeal—a magnetism—that allows them to successfully influence everyone around them. You know who they are. They are individuals you see on television, read about in newspapers, or possibly run into at the office. It is time to join them.

Alicia Silverstone Isn't the Only One Who's Clueless

If you work in sales, research shows your number-one pain point is making quota. It should be. Miss your numbers and you are out of a job. However, for many sales managers, a close second to making quota is motivating the people they supervise. Unfortunately, most people are clueless when it comes to inspiring others. I read an interview in the *New York Times* with an event planner, recounting some of the horror stories she experienced on the job. At one conference she coordinated, a company president organized a stunt as a "motivational" tool. The president, an expert archer, picked his top saleswoman from the audience and asked her to balance an apple on her head so he could shoot an arrow through it from fifty feet![1] The arrow hit its target and the saleswoman survived, but the president was way off the mark. In this book, you will not learn corny gimmicks to fire up your sales team. You *will* learn how to speak with confidence, and by doing so, you will inspire everyone, including yourself.

Be Like Apple. Think Different

In his book, *Hope: How Triumphant Leaders Create the Future*, Andrew Razeghi quotes a study that found "only 20 percent of all U.S. employees want to be with their current employer in two years."[2] What's truly alarming is that most employees cite a lack of leadership as their reason for going elsewhere. Today's workers crave meaning in their lives and a professional role that represents something larger than themselves. Unfortunately, few leaders communicate meaning, hope, and optimism. They fail to create an emotional connection with their employees, customers, and colleagues. But you have an opportunity to be different, to excel, and to inspire others in a way you have yet to imagine.

Bad, Boring, and Blah or Energizing, Engaging, and Electric!

As a journalist and communications coach, I come across three types of communicators.

THE CHIEF OF BLAH

This person does not consider the need to inspire his employees as part of his job description. A meeting is simply an opportunity to announce an order; a presentation is a way to score points, to show his superiors that he should keep his job. Nothing more. His primary goal is to keep bringing in his paycheck and to get a bigger bonus than his colleagues. He is not inspiring, nor does he want to be. Instead of energizing, he extinguishes, snuffing out all creativity, energy, and drive in the people around him.

THE CHIEF OF MEDIOCRITY

This person is genuinely concerned about the need to rally her team, but she does not have the tools to match the power of her communications with her desire. She does an adequate job of communicating her mission, but she could be clearer, more convincing, and more compelling. This is the kind of person who can make enjoyable small talk at the company barbecue, but nobody is eager to join her at work on Monday morning.

THE CHIEF INSPIRATION OFFICER

This person is an extraordinary communicator. He places a strong emphasis on the way he crafts and delivers his message, vision, and values. He is successful at getting listeners actually to change what they have come to believe. He successfully rallies people around the vivid future he sees and helps them find meaning in their roles. This leader is magnetic. He leaves everyone energized, enthusiastic, and electrified!

Your existing title is irrelevant. The only thing that matters is that you want to be more captivating and confident in the way you speak, because in this book, you'll learn from the best. In Chapter One, you will meet one entrepreneur whose title is "Grand Poo Bah." He has an untraditional title but a remarkable ability to electrify the people around him. Don't sweat the title. Achieve results. Your title will take care of itself.

Enchant the Soul

The standard definition of "rhetoric" is the art of persuasion through language. I prefer Plato's take on it: the art of enchanting the soul. Enchant the soul of your listeners, and you will enjoy influence, success, and joy beyond your wildest dreams.

The Real Hell's Kitchen

Like most people, I have worked for some managers whose failure to communicate effectively left everyone in the division or company uninspired, unmotivated, and demoralized. I spent a couple of years under one boss who made Chef Gordon Ramsey on the Fox show *Hell's Kitchen* look as friendly as a puppy in a pet store. This particular manager was a well-known television personality who tried on a boss's hat for a few years. Not a good idea. When he got mad, he would yell for his supervisors, bring them into his office—which was within earshot of my mine—slam the door shut, and scream obscenities for two hours. Grown men would walk out with tears in their eyes. Working for this monster—uh, "manager"—motivated me to leave that particular job and live my life on my own terms; I choose my own path, I'm my own boss, and I avoid working for people who fail to lift the spirits of those around them. This manager "motivated" out of fear but failed to inspire.

You do not need a book to teach you how to act like a jerk. Poor managers think that motivation means scaring the heck out of people. It doesn't. Other managers think we're all like Pavlov's dogs: Give us a treat and we'll perform. These managers believe that offering incentives, such as a 50-inch widescreen plasma TV for the person with the highest sales, is all the motivation his team needs. It's not. Financial or material incentives might work for a few hours or days, but they will fail to inspire people over the long run.

Many leaders have yet to discover this basic fact: Fewer than half of U.S. workers are happy with their jobs, and only 14 percent are "very satisfied," according to a Conference Board survey.[3] This low level of engagement costs the American economy an estimated $350 billion a year in lost productivity.[4] I could offer more statistics, but why bother? Clearly, people are desperate for inspiring leadership. We all know it. Just look at the frown on the face of the person next to you on the train Monday morning, the demeanor of the bank teller, the lack of enthusiasm and customer service skills from the sales clerk at the department store. People are uninspired, and it shows. Keep this in mind as you read the stories of the inspiring individuals in this book;

although you may work for a demoralizing boss, you can choose to be different. You can choose to join the men and women who are among the most influential people on the planet, capturing the hearts and minds of everyone you meet. As an old saying goes, when you are ready, the teacher will appear. The teachers are in this book, so get ready!

I encourage you to be the type of person people want to stick with for the long term, the person whose vision people want to follow, and the person who brings out the best in others. Your customers, colleagues, clients, employees, staff, team, students, and children are searching for someone to satisfy their chief want. If you miss the opportunity to engage them, they will look elsewhere for inspiration: another company, a competitor, a boss, a congregation, or, saddest of all, questionable peers. We all want to be around someone who makes us feel good about ourselves and engages our hearts and minds with the vision of a brighter future. You have the ability and, I would argue, the obligation, to play this role for those in your life. All you need are the right tools, the proper insight, and a dose of motivation from others who have achieved this extraordinary level of influence.

A Simple Formula for Career Success

If you truly want to make a mark in this world—to leave a "ding in the universe," as Apple cofounder Steve Jobs once said—then you must elevate your personal brand and become a person of influence who communicates with confidence and charisma. Not only will you be rewarded on a personal level, but your career and company will reap the benefits. Engaged employees are passionate, innovative, and exceed their sales targets. They value their organization and, most important, their immediate supervisor or manager. According to a study by Watson Wyatt Worldwide, companies whose leaders communicate successfully also outperform their competitors financially; companies with highly effective communications practices had a level of employee engagement that was nearly five times greater than that of the competition.[5] Those companies also posted a significantly higher return to shareholders over a five-year period.

According to leadership professor and author Jay Conger, "A more educated, more intrinsically motivated workplace demands that executives and managers recast their image more in the light of an effective political leader. They must learn to sell themselves and their missions—this depends on highly effective language skills."[6] In the future, says Conger, "leaders will not only have to be effective strategists, but rhetoricians who can energize through the words they choose. The era of managing by dictate is ending and is being replaced by an era of managing by inspiration." Think about it. Management by inspiration. What a glorious goal!

You might want listeners to enthusiastically embrace your vision for the company, buy your product, or choose your service. Reaching these goals requires that you build an emotional connection between your listeners and your vision, your brand, and yourself. When you succeed at creating that connection, the results are magical, leading to a transformation in your life as well as contributing to positive change in those around you. The people around you are looking for meaning, belonging, and a sense of fulfillment but are not getting it. You can change that, and you must, to enjoy a richer life. Adopt the 7 Simple Secrets and people will walk through walls for you.

Inspire!

This book is based on observations and interviews with dozens of extraordinary men and women who communicate visions that are irrepressible, irresistible, and wildly contagious. If you are ready to take your place among them, the 7 Simple Secrets will take you there. The next seven chapters in Part I will put you on the road to becoming a super motivator. Get ready to INSPIRE:

1. Ignite Your Enthusiasm: Light a Fire in Your Heart before Sparking One in Theirs.
2. Navigate the Way: Deliver a Specific, Consistent, and Memorable Vision.
3. Sell the Benefit: Put Your Listeners First.
4. Paint a Picture: Tell Powerful, Memorable, and Actionable Stories.
5. Invite Participation: Solicit Input, Overcome Objections, and Develop a Winning Strategy.
6. Reinforce an Optimistic Outlook: Become a Beacon of Hope.
7. Encourage People to Reach Their Potential: Praise People, Invest in Them, and Unleash Their Potential.

Part I explores each of the 7 Simple Secrets in detail. Part II includes conversations and observations of inspiring individuals in different fields. These chapters will help you to appreciate the wide range of situations in which you can apply the secrets.

Inspiring communicators have nailed the 7 Simple Secrets. By doing so, they leave people energized, enthusiastic, and motivated. When you are in the presence of these extraordinary individuals, you are left with the belief—the absolutely certain belief—that everything you have ever wanted to achieve is possible. They make you feel better about yourself and the world in which we all do business. They embrace change. They love challenge. They fill their days with positive energy and see a future that is bright and hopeful. This collective energy results in a motivated, positive, energized workplace, proven to increase the value of the organization. You have the potential to exert positive influence on the lives of those around you. These 7 Simple Secrets will allow you to take your rightful place among the world's most inspiring leaders.

Inspiration comes in many forms. I am inspired by the radiant smile of my baby daughter when she sees her daddy in the morning, the par-3 seventeenth hole at Pebble Beach, and the emerald-blue water of Lake Tahoe. Accomplishments inspire us, too. We can be inspired by the deeds of extraordinary men and women, both historical and contemporary: Napoleon Bonaparte, Martin Luther King Jr., Oprah Winfrey, Bill Gates, and other innovative minds. Few of us will live at a confluence of history where we can unleash previously untapped powers to change the world, but we are all catalysts of change for the people around us. We all strive to improve our existence, to be our best selves, and to leave a legacy, but most of us need an extra push, someone to inspire us. It is our chief want, and this book will show you how to satisfy it. Now let's get started.

CHAPTER 1

Ignite Your Enthusiasm

Light a Fire in Your Heart before Sparking One in Theirs

> This is the one true joy in life, the being used for a purpose
> recognized by yourself as a mighty one.
>
> —George Bernard Shaw

In the 2006 season of *America's Next Top Model,* supermodel Tyra Banks and her zany cast of judges faced a decision: whether to advance one of two twin sisters competing for the ultimate prize of a cover shoot for *Seventeen* magazine and $100,000 to jump-start her career. Michelle had poise, grace, and technical skills. Her sister, Amanda, lacked Michelle's natural talent but wanted it more. Amanda was enthusiastic about modeling and wanted nothing less than to make it her life's calling. Michelle, however, admitted that she did not have the same energy and passion as her sister or the other candidates. "In this competition, passion is way more important than beautiful pictures," said Tyra as she eliminated Michelle. Likewise, in the competition to inspire listeners, passion and excitement will separate you from the pack. Energize yourself before you attempt to engage the hearts and minds of your audience.

In my role as a communications coach, I meet astonishing business professionals in a cross section of industries and roles: in the executive ranks, sales, marketing, and throughout all levels of the organization. The most energizing among them have a personal quality that lifts everyone's spirit. They are a tiny but bright constellation, a group of star performers who are worlds away from the majority of leaders in business today. While they share 7 Simple Secrets that set them apart, it all starts with one common thread, Simple Secret #1: Successful leaders are fired up about what they do and have an extraordinary ability to generate excitement in others.

How One Google Executive Found Her Field of Dreams

Inspiration begins internally. What is it about your service, product, company, or cause that pumps you up? Only after you identify what you are truly passionate about will you be in a position to motivate others. Marissa Mayer is the Vice President of Search Products for Google. She has her hands on pretty much every feature that appears on the search engine: colors, graphics, tools, and interfaces. Her role impacts the Internet searches that millions of people conduct daily. But it's her passion that got her there.

You might not expect a computer science major to have a warm, friendly, and outgoing personality, and I say that with only the greatest affection for technologists, but when I first met Mayer, she shattered my stereotype. She had recently been featured on the cover of several magazines, including *Newsweek* and *Fast Company*. She is articulate and has striking good looks (she captained the pom-pom squad for her high school in Wausau, Wisconsin, but I doubt her cheerleading experience makes it to the top of her resume). Mayer works an insane number of hours. Her weekdays begin at 9:00 a.m. and end at 8:00 p.m. Those are only the hours she spends in the office. After hitting the

Google gym around 11:00 p.m., she typically answers email until 3:00 a.m.! And you thought you spent a lot of time at work.

Mayer has found a career that ignites her passion for how technology can improve our lives. "I'm amazed at the role Google plays in the world today," she says. "Touching people's lives and giving them information to choose better jobs, take better educational paths, find better medical treatment. Information is fundamentally critical."[1]

In one respect, the information Mayer leaves out of the conversation is more important than what she includes. She never says a word about money, stock, the gym, or the famous Google cafeteria. (The company employs gourmet chefs to serve up fancy, delicious, and free meals to its employees. When was the last time you found Eggplant Ratatouille, Seared Day Boat Scallops in a Green Coconut Curry Sauce, or Tropical Shrimp Bisque Soup in your company kitchen?) There is no question that a good salary, health benefits, a club membership, a cafeteria, and free coffee are nice perks, but while perks keep us coming back to the office, they do not inspire. Big difference. Mayer's teams of engineers and product managers enjoy working with her because her enthusiasm is infectious. She makes them feel good about the company, its products, and the role those products play in the world today. "In 1982, we had a lot of space where I grew up in Wisconsin," Mayer recalls, "and I remember me and my group of friends had planned to build an actual baseball diamond. Was it 88 feet between bases or 90? we asked. We reached an impasse because we didn't want to ask our parents to drive us to the library, pull out a reference book, and look it up. That was the only way to answer that question back then. Today you just type it into Google and have an answer immediately."

According to Mayer, you would be hard-pressed to find a group of individuals who make a larger contribution to the world than her colleagues at Google. She communicates this enthusiasm in conversations, meetings, emails, and presentations. "People need to appreciate the impact they are having," says Mayer. "When you produce a product that is installed on tens of millions of machines or viewed tens of millions of times across the world, you have an impact on people's lives. You have a serious responsibility to users and the world."

Mayer creates a strong emotional connection to her listeners because she is deeply committed to the message. She exudes energy, enthusiasm, and excitement. You must do the same. Once you make a positive association between yourself and the message, you are more likely to reach the holy grail of influence: turning listeners into evangelists. Evangelists have such a deep passion for you, your brand, and your message that they will sing your praises to others. John Watson Sr., the founder of IBM, said, "The great accomplishments of man have resulted from the transmission of enthusiasm." Transmit enthusiasm. Do great things.

How a Pop Star Washed Out the Cobwebs

People find inspiration in many ways. One of my clients, Latin pop star Obie Bermudez, found inspiration in a South Bronx laundry. His first album garnered very little attention, certainly not enough to let him live the life of a superstar. To make a living, he worked in a Laundromat for five years. Watching the daily interactions of the customers inspired him to write nearly all the songs for his second album, which reached number one on the Latin music charts. The spin cycle actually helped him find his voice!

How the Brain behind Cranium Connects with Your Heart

When I stepped out of the elevator into Cranium's colorful office space near Seattle's famed Pike Place Market, I was hit with a wave of energy, enthusiasm, and excitement that I had rarely experienced in corporate

Figure 1.1 Cranium's infectious enthusiasm affects everyone; Cranium's "Professor Profit," Jack Lawrence, takes a lap around the office on his scooter to celebrate a "financial milestone."
Photo by Ken Lambert, May 28, 2006. Photo courtesy of *The Seattle Times*.

America. These people really love their jobs, I thought. Everyone greets you like you are their best friend. They smile through the gloomiest Seattle day. (See Figure 1.1.) A sense of pride permeates their conversations. Cranium has successfully reinvented the board game category, creating the fastest-selling independent board game in history. It has become more than a game; it is a place that unleashes the limitless creativity and energy of its employees, who create award-winning games, toys, and books that are so infectious, buyers call themselves "Craniacs." Where does this energy come from? I wondered. I did not have to look far. Sitting in a glass-walled office filled with toys and games was Cranium's inventor Richard Tait, one of the most awe-inspiring entrepreneurs in America today.

I was about to get my first dose of the dynamic Scot whom Bill Gates had once selected as Microsoft's Employee of the Year. Richard Tait is now Cranium's cofounder, or "Grand Poo Bah." No kidding. That is his title. In fact, everyone at Cranium is encouraged to come up with a title that fits their job description. The "Head of the Hive" oversees publicity, or buzz. The "Chief Culture Keeper" heads HR, and the "Concierge" is the receptionist. You get the idea. Everything about Cranium is intended to reinvent the rules of how business is conducted. It is not often that I meet a charismatic pitchman like Tait. "Within five minutes of meeting Tait, you'll want to work for him," a colleague told me. She was right. Tait's energy and enthusiasm are wildly infectious. He is an entrepreneur, inventor, leader, and *Chief Inspiration Officer* for Cranium's employees, investors, and customers.

After ten years at Microsoft, where he specialized in starting new businesses, Tait left the company to create something of his own. He was determined to build a company that would delight customers around the world. However, he had yet to find a project that would ignite his enthusiasm. He certainly never thought that he would find success in a board game, especially one that requires players to answer trivia questions, whistle tunes, act out characters, or play with clay! But on a trip out East, this man from the West created a game that would unite friends and families around the world.

During a vacation with friends in the Hamptons, Tait and his wife, Karen, were playing their favorite board game, Pictionary. "Karen and I were unbeaten. We dusted them at Pictionary," Tait told me during our interview.[2] "Our friends wanted revenge, so they challenged us to a game of Scrabble. Scrabble is a word that can send shivers down my spine even to this day. Our friends are demons at Scrabble. Sure enough, they humbled us," said Tait, who blamed himself for the defeat. The loss did not lead to an aha moment as much as it left Tait with a feeling of looking like an idiot in front of his family and friends. The defining moment hit him on the plane ride home to Seattle. What if a game existed that had something for all players, where everyone had a chance to shine, to show off a special talent and be celebrated for that skill? "What would a game like that *feel* like? It would have to be a game that had performance challenges, data and trivia challenges, language and word puzzles, and creative activities. I sketched out the idea for the game on a napkin."

On that flight, Cranium was born. I italicized "feel" in Tait's quote because the word is a recurring theme in my interviews with inspiring business leaders. It tells me that these individuals are affected emotionally by the products and services they create, pitch, or sell. They generate excitement in others because they are deeply passionate themselves.

The Napkin Test

Most venture capitalists would laugh you out of the room if you showed up with a business plan on a piece of paper you just used to wipe the blueberry pancake stain off your mouth. So why do so many companies seem to take shape on the back of a napkin? Simplicity. Cranium's Richard Tait once gave a presentation after writing seven points on the back of a business card. Charismatic communicators make their message easy to grasp. The most exciting messages are memorable, repeatable, and strikingly simple.

INFECTIOUS ENTHUSIASM

When Tait returned to Seattle from his trip to the Hamptons, he pitched the idea to a Microsoft friend, Whit Alexander, now Cranium's "Chief Noodler." At the time, Alexander was less than eager to tell his parents that he had left the world's most important technology company to create a board game that encouraged players to whistle the tune to

Star Wars or sculpt Medusa out of clay. But Tait's enthusiasm was hard to ignore.

Although Tait and Alexander had an abundance of enthusiasm, they were not satisfied. Cranium would take off only if they managed to persuade retailers to carry it. The two were off to a bad start—or so they thought—when they missed launching the game at the Toy Fair, a major show where retailers decide what toys to stock for the coming year. Tait and Alexander decided to drink away their woes. But instead of heading to a bar, they settled on the fine Seattle tradition of meeting at Starbucks. The decision they made over lattes that day would change their lives forever. Looking around, the two men realized that they were surrounded by the type of customers who would enjoy Cranium. "Let's take our game to where our customers are instead of where games are traditionally sold," they decided. That's the magic of passion—doors appear that would otherwise go unnoticed.

The Cranium guys had such an abundance of enthusiasm, they would soon win over a key player in their success, Starbucks founder Howard Schultz. He liked the game but also appreciated the power of enthusiasm to infect employees and customers. Schultz is all about infectious enthusiasm, which is why he thinks employees should be treated exceptionally well: Happy employees are enthusiastic, and that translates into superior customer service. It's a simple formula. The brains behind Cranium had won over a key distributor and one that would jump-start its rocket ride to success. Cranium became the first board game carried at Starbucks.

Fueled by the passion of its two partners, Cranium took off. Celebrities jumped on board. The company did not need to advertise when Hollywood biggies like Julia Roberts were raving about it on *Oprah*. Cranium sold 10,000 copies in its first holiday season. Today Cranium has sold more than 16 million copies of its games. In February 2007, the Toy Industry Association awarded Cranium its coveted Toy of the Year in the games category; it was the fifth time Cranium had won the award. Cranium has expanded into spin-off games, books, and award-winning toys. Cranium's journey to cult-like status began with a trip, an aha moment, and an abundance of enthusiasm.

LEAVING A FOOTPRINT IN THE SAND

Military leaders know that motivation is contagious. If one person is fired up, it rubs off on the next person and the next. Once everyone on the team shares the excitement, they all perform better together. The same is true of teams on the corporate battlefield. Richard Tait saw the delight in the eyes of his customers the moment he sketched the concept for Cranium on the back of a napkin. That is where it would have remained had it not been for Tait's willingness to share that excitement with anyone who would listen—beginning with his cofounder and expanding to partners, employees, and customers.

"What inspires you?" I asked Tait.

First and foremost, it's the letters from customers I read every night before I go to bed. [Tait reads more than one hundred customer stories a day.] That gives me the strength and the belief that tomorrow we have to bring more of these moments into people's lives. The woman who wrote me at 11:30 one night—she has four kids of her own and three foster children. Instead of kicking her feet up at the end of a long day and enjoying a glass of wine, she's writing to tell me about the sense of togetherness our games bring to her family, a family previously fragmented and separated by age, ethnicities, and backgrounds. This woman is writing at 11:30 at night to thank me for creating these products. When is the last time you wrote to a company, thanking them for creating a product? I don't know about you, but I've never done it in my life. One of our core values as a company is to delight our customers at every turn. Those moments of delight inspire me everyday.

"How do you share that enthusiasm with your colleagues? How do you get them pumped up around the same ideals?" I asked.

We share stories from our customers avidly within company. They are posted around the environment. [Stories, letters, and photographs are even placed under countertops throughout the office space.] When I read a story, I'll send it in an email and talk about it in our company meetings. You need to show the difference everyone makes in people's lives. Our employees have the opportunity to make history. In today's world, those opportunities are few and far between. They have a real chance to be a part of something special. They'll be able to look back with their kids or grandkids and say, I was a part of that. In today's world, people are looking for a footprint in the sand. If there is an opportunity to leave it as part of a team and organization that is doing good work, then it's a powerful promise to the folks who work here.

Our world needs fewer managers and more Grand Poo Bahs. We all want to leave a footprint in the sand. You can inspire others to take those first steps.

Cranium's Secret Sauce

By Richard Tait, Cranium "Grand Poo Bah"

- *Have a clear sense of mission.* Make it relevant, easy to understand, and something that people are passionate about and that they rally around.
- *Create a culture and celebrate it every day.* Identify what makes your culture and organization special. What are the principles and values that you want people to embrace? Create methods of celebrating and reinforcing that culture. Make it your own, make it special, and make it an environment that people are proud to be a part of.

▮ *Don't be afraid to change the rules; in fact, encourage it and celebrate it.* The best way to win the game is to change how it is being played in a way that works to your advantage. Provide a culture and work environment that supports and celebrates those well-calculated risks.

▮ *Your customers are your sales force.* Our company's success has been built on word-of-mouth as a marketing vehicle. We must never forget that Craniacs are fueling our growth, and every interaction that they have with our company must result in a sense of delight and enthusiasm, a pride of association that encourages them to introduce and include their friends and family in our brand.

▮ *Be a company with a heart.* From the very beginning we wanted to be a company with a heart, one that our employees and customers would be proud of and one that would extend our brand purpose to lighten and enlighten people's lives, beyond the purchase of our products.

▮ *Lead by example.* I try to lead with speed, passion, and a sense of discovery. My personal mantra is that Orville Wright did not have a pilot's license. I hope that each and every Cranium employee feels a sense of freedom and empowerment to embrace these qualities and apply them to their own individual contributions, to feel that their ideas are listened to and supported and that they should champion them with enthusiasm, and to feel supported when trying new ways to solve problems or create opportunities.

Are you beginning to see a trend here? Both Mayer and Tait succeed in energizing their colleagues by sharing their enthusiasm in all their professional communications. Employees who work for the companies featured in this book do not see themselves as dispensable cogs in a soulless corporation. Instead they see themselves as playing key roles on a dream team of sorts, a team bringing hope, light, and promise to those they touch. They are leaving a "footprint in the sand," as Tait said—stories they will proudly tell future generations. Mayer and Tait are leaders in every sense—in title, spirit, and attitude. But remember, you do not need a leadership title to influence those around you. Just as I sat down to begin writing this book, I ran into one of the most inspiring women I had ever met. She does not "lead" a company, but her enthusiasm wins over the hearts of hundreds of employees and customers every week.

Driving Enthusiasm

Krista Hawkins fires up hundreds of potential customers every week. She is not an executive, a manager, or a saleswoman. Hawkins is a tour guide—one of the most passionate, excited, and enthusiastic guides you have ever seen. Where would you expect to find someone like this? SeaWorld? Nope. Disneyland? Not quite. She lives two thousand miles from the Magic Kingdom, but Hawkins works her personal magic on everyone she meets. Hawkins gives tours of a car plant in Montgomery, Alabama. Not just any car plant: Hyundai Motors Manufacturing, one of the most technically advanced facilities in the world. In the heart of the American South, Korean-owned Hyundai turns out eleven hundred cars a day for the North American market. The majority of cars manufactured at the plant are the Santa Fe (an SUV) and the midsize Sonata, both of which are among Hyundai's best-selling models, winning rave reviews for safety, quality, and value. Meanwhile, Hawkins is winning over a legion of customers: some three hundred people per week who tour the plant. Her enthusiasm turns visitors into customers and customers into evangelists.

I met Hawkins at a conference, where I spoke to Hyundai marketing and advertising executives about the need for each and every one of them to be passionate spokespeople for their brand. During lunch on the hotel terrace, I overheard Hawkins talk about her job with such passion and enthusiasm that I could not help but strike up a conversation. Hawkins was riveting, and I asked her to stand and say a few words during my lecture. Her enthusiasm spread immediately. When she was finished, everyone in the audience cheered, clapped, and smiled. "My point exactly!" I exclaimed. Everyone who works for a brand represents it to the outside world. Every interaction is an opportunity to put a face to the brand—a face that must be wildly enthusiastic, energized, and engaged if you hope to win over your listeners. (See Figure 1.2.)

"I never dread going to work," Hawkins told me.[3]

I have a smile on my face every day. I find something as simple as a smile to be infectious. I greet everyone with a smile. If I can read the name on their shirt, I will greet them by name. If you've come off the line after working four hours, it's great to be met with a smile and enthusiasm. It lifts your spirits. I started in Human Resources and interviewed for production line positions. I saw how Hyundai changed the lives of our team members and their families. I also see what the plant has done for the community and the state of Alabama. How can you not be happy? I've never had a bad day here.

Imagine working side by side with an employee like Hawkins every day. Her greeting alone would help you shake off the early morning alarm, the long train ride to work, or missing your first cup of coffee. Every company needs a Hawkins. But listen closely to what excites her. Hawkins sees her role as an opportunity to leave visitors with a positive impression of the brand and the men and women behind it.

Figure 1.2 Passion sells cars at Hyundai's state of the art plant in Montgomery, Alabama; "Thumbs Up!"
Author unknown, 2005, photo courtesy of Hyundai Motor Manufacturing, Alabama.

She never uses the term "employees." To Hawkins, everyone is a "team member." Although she appreciates the quality of the cars, Hawkins is not excited about the leather seats, wood trim, or aluminum-alloy wheels. It is not the product that inspires her, but what the product has done for the lives of employees and customers.

Hawkins is especially pumped up about the role Hyundai plays in the lives of the men and women who assemble the cars. According to Hawkins, "Our team is a family. Despite the fact that this plant is the most technologically advanced in the world, teamwork plays a big part in the quality of a car. Everyone has to perform their task perfectly, and that requires communication with your teammates down the line. Everyone's mind has to be in it one hundred percent."

ROBOTS DON'T HIGH-FIVE

I know it might seem odd to say this about a manufacturing plant, but the Hyundai tour is cool. More than 250 robots begin the process of stamping (cutting steel), welding, and painting. Robot arms suspend and manipulate the car's shell as the steel is turned 360 degrees and dunked eleven times into special baths to apply coatings and paints. Robots are exciting to watch, but the real thrill happens during the general assembly when cheerful, smiling, high-fiving teams of one thousand human beings install the parts of each vehicle, including the wiring, brakes, engines, tires, doors, seats, and glass. Conveying enthusiasm is a quality robots have not quite mastered.

"The tours give me the opportunity to share the story behind our quality," says Hawkins. "The quality of our vehicles is directly related to the energy of our people. There's a lot of positive energy in our plant. That energy is going to translate into quality because everyone is passionate about the roles they play in building your car." Hawkins is convinced that the enthusiasm that rubs off on each and every team member has helped the company build cars that have leapfrogged their rivals in terms of quality, safety, and customer satisfaction. Hawkins does not start a tour with the purpose of selling cars. Her goal is to entertain and inform visitors about how teamwork creates quality. But given the number of hugs she gets from visitors—yes, hugs—she might very well be Hyundai's best salesperson!

The three Es must permeate every level of an organization: Energy, Enthusiasm and Excitement. Although you may not be the face of a company on CNBC, when you communicate with potential customers, you are the sole experience they have with the brand at that moment. Whether you answer phones, make sales pitches, or give tours, the way you communicate speaks volumes about two brands:

the company's brand and your own. What is the customer's experience like? When you talk to customers or colleagues, do they leave that conversation inspired, energized, and enthusiastic or uninspired, disillusioned, and bored? That is up to you.

The View from the Top

In *What It Takes to Be #1*, Vince Lombardi Jr., writes that his father—the football legend who led the Green Bay Packers to five championships—delivered his pep talks with a missionary zeal, intended to grab hearts and minds. "Embrace your passion," Lombardi would say. "Jump into your passion with both feet and bring others along with you." According to Lombardi Jr., his dad taught him this important lesson: "Passion and enthusiasm are the seeds of achievement. Enthusiasm is like an ocean tide. There's a certain inevitability about it. Passion sweeps away obstacles. To motivate people, there must be a spark, some juice, desire, inspiration. It's tough to be a leader if you can't energize your people and tap into their emotional energy."[4]

Pump 'Em Up the Jack Welch Way

"Leaders have always had to energize their people," says former General Electric CEO Jack Welch.[5] In today's fiercely competitive global economy, Welch believes that it's more important than ever for leaders to inspire everyone around them if they hope to compete. "[Leaders] have to pump up their people to tackle unscaleable heights and make them understand why change is constantly necessary, passionately explaining what's in it for the company—and employees," writes Welch in *BusinessWeek*. "No company, large or small, can win over the long run without energized employees who believe in the mission and understand how to achieve it."

Whether your role is that of a CEO, manager, sales leader, or receptionist, the enthusiasm behind what you do will make all the difference in the ultimate success of your company and your career. According to Welch, it is common to find smart, capable people whose careers are stalled because they fail to win over their employees, investors, customers, and colleagues. Do not let your career sputter, stall, and die. Infuse your conversations and presentations with energy, enthusiasm, and excitement. Doing so will help you win over the hearts and minds of your listeners.

The Secret Behind Trump's Success

Millions of people want to be like Donald Trump. They buy his books, watch his television shows, pay hundreds of dollars for a ticket to watch him speak, and even drink his water (yes, there really is Trump bottled water). They hope Trump will offer a nugget of information that they can spin into gold. But when you strip away the buildings, the mansions, the jets, the helicopters, and listen to him—I mean really *listen* to his message—Trump's secret to success is simple: Do what you love. On CNN's *Larry King Live,* a caller once asked Trump what made him a great negotiator—again, someone looking for that special something that will turn his fortunes around. Trump responded, "You have to love what you do and you should never, ever give up. But, if you don't love it, then you will give up easier. Love what you do."[6]

The Lovable Star

Donald Trump once said, "Without passion you don't have energy. Without energy, you have nothing." By feeling inspired yourself, you will have boundless energy, enthusiasm and excitement—all of those qualities that you make likable; and if people like you, they are more likely to buy into your vision and your values.

When given a chance to work for someone, who would you prefer—a person who knows a lot but who acts like a jackass, or someone who is both smart and *likable*? If you are reading this book, it is not much of a stretch to guess that you prefer the latter. Most people do. According to a Harvard Business School study, researchers concluded that "if someone is strongly disliked, it's almost irrelevant whether or not she is competent; people won't want to work for her anyway. By contrast, if someone is liked, his colleagues will seek out every little bit of competence he has to offer. And this tendency didn't exist only in extreme cases; it was true across the board. Generally speaking, a little extra likeability goes a longer way than a little extra competence in making someone desirable to work with."[7] This research is highly relevant to the topic of inspiration because if your listeners do not like you, it becomes that much tougher to establish an emotional connection with them. When we are in the presence of people we like, we are more likely to follow the vision they articulate.

I recall having a conversation with a highly successful mutual fund manager in New York. When I asked what he looks for in a company, he replied, "I invest in people I trust." Yes, the business model needs to show promise, but this fund manager said if he doesn't like someone, he will not invest in the company. Savvy investors don't put their money in buildings, but in the people *behind* the buildings.

A heavy dose of likability is a key ingredient in the motivation recipe. The men and women featured in this book are likable on a personal level before they win over their listeners in a professional setting. Think about it: Do you connect with your employees, investors, customers, or colleagues on a deep level? Do they like you? Do they trust you? How you communicate your values makes all the difference; the road to becoming a master communicator begins with the passion, energy, and enthusiasm you bring to your story.

**Embrace Your Passion and Enthusiasm
Will Follow**

When testing your own personal vision, first ask yourself: Does the vision tap into my voice, my energy, my unique talent? Does it give me a sense of "calling," a cause worthy of my commitment?
—Stephen R. Covey, Author, The 7 Habits of Highly Successful People[8]

"If you love something, you'll be great at it, the money will come, and everything else will fall into place.
— Donny Deutsch, advertising mogul and host of CNBC's *The Big Idea with Donny Deutsch*[9]

THE BEAUTY IN A HAMBURGER BUN

Legendary business titan Ray Kroc, who created the McDonald's franchise system, once said, "It requires a certain kind of mind to see beauty in a hamburger bun." What do you see in the product or service your company provides or makes? Do you see its beauty, its ability to improve the lives of its customers and employees? The McDonald's franchise thrived under the Kroc's leadership; his enthusiasm rubbed off on the franchise owners. Owners became evangelists and spread the company gospel, fueling the brand's growth.

Enthusiasm separates average performers from extraordinary leaders. Leaders who wow their listeners are excited and energized about the role they play in the company and the industry and in the lives of their customers. They are advocates for the brand. If Kroc could find the beauty in a hamburger bun, you can certainly find something exciting about your brand.

We all want to be surrounded by people who have an unbridled enthusiasm for life. The death of Australia's Crocodile Hunter, Steve Irwin, touched millions of people around the world because his passion for what he did—for wildlife and conservation—was obvious in every interview and television show. His energy jumped off the screen. We love to be around passionate people. Their energy is contagious, and there is something magical about being in their presence. Business professionals, entrepreneurs, coaches, parents, teachers, and leaders in every walk of life have to be fired up about what they do in order to inspire the people around them.

Inspiring individuals like Marissa Mayer, Richard Tait, and Krista Hawkins succeed in creating a culture of innovation by lighting a fire in the hearts of their colleagues and employees—a desire to change the world not by the products they create, but by what the products do for their customers. "Rarely in life are you given the chance to fly, to feel the passion and pursuit of something special, a dream," says Tait. What dreams do you have? How do you communicate those dreams? You have no limitations except those of your own imagination. Dream big, get fired up about those dreams, and watch as others want to come along for the ride!

CHAPTER 2

Navigate the Way

Deliver a Specific, Consistent, and Memorable Vision

> A leader succeeds only when they find a way to make people excited and confident in what comes next.
> —Marcus Buckingham,
> The One Thing You Need to Know

Enthusiasm opens the door, but vision grabs hold of your listeners and pulls them to the other side. In this chapter you will learn Simple Secret #2, the one secret that can give you instant charisma. Extraordinary leaders, managers, entrepreneurs, educators, and sales professionals have mastered this one ability, and so will you. The secret is this: Create an emotional connection with an audience by articulating a vision so bright, so magnificent, the rest of us cannot help but come along for the ride.

Marcus Buckingham studied management, leadership, and productivity at the Gallup organization for seventeen years. After interviewing thousands of peak performers over the course of his career, he arrived at what he considers the single best definition of leadership:

"Great leaders rally people to a better future," he writes in *The One Thing You Need to Know*.[1] According to Buckingham, a leader carries a vivid image in his head of what a future could be. "Leaders are fascinated by the future. You are a leader if, and only if, you are restless for change, impatient for progress and deeply dissatisfied with the status quo. . . . As a leader, you are never satisfied with the present, because in your head you can see a better future, and the friction between 'what is' and 'what could be' burns you, stirs you up, propels you forward. This is leadership."[2]

It is important to recognize that by Buckingham's definition, most of us play a leadership role every day. How you speak in this role will determine your ultimate success. A sales manager who demonstrates how her product saves money and boosts productivity is a leader who rallies her prospects to a better future. A financial advisor who recommends the right mix of stocks and bonds to help an individual meet his goals is a leader who rallies his clients to a better future. A franchise owner who inspires staff to offer mind-blowing service is a leader who rallies employees and customers to a better future. In order to propel your personal brand to new heights, you must be able to articulate the goal you are trying to achieve, a goal that is specific, consistent, and memorable.

Creating Excitement at GE

Leaders who succeed at retaining their best employees "constantly create excitement in their groups," says Jack Welch in a *BusinessWeek* article.[3] "They need to be aspirational, explaining why the team's mission is important, and inspirational, talking frequently and personally with top performers about their individual routes to success." Welch's successor, Jeffrey Immelt, also considers setting a course the role of a leader. In an article for *Fast Company*, he said the number-one goal for a chief executive or any leader is to constantly communicate the mission, goals, and purpose of the company. "We have a generation of people who know how to do process flow charts. We have a generation of people who know how to do quality function deployment and things like that, but don't necessarily know why they're doing them. What's the what and the where?"[4]

A fuzzy vision will fail to rally your listeners to a better future. In one of my favorite Dilbert cartoons, Dilbert's boss asks a young job candidate, "Can you work well without supervision?" The wide-eyed recruit eagerly responds, "Yes! I thrive on vague objectives and a complete lack of recognition for my contribution."[5] Unfortunately, this happens all too often—most business leaders either do not have a vision (don't laugh, it's true) or fail to convey it clearly. This is all the more reason for us to study the men and women who do light a fire in our hearts through the clear articulation of an exciting vision.

Avoid Confusion

Do not confuse vision with a mission statement. A mission statement is a long, convoluted paragraph, drafted by multiple teams of C-suite executives, vice presidents, and directors over the course of hours or days that is destined to be posted somewhere in the office but largely forgotten. I have never met an executive or employee who has been able to recite the company's mission statement. I ask all the time just for a kick. It never happens.

If you must create a mission statement to satisfy some deep-seated corporate guilt, then make it easy on yourself by using a ready-made "mission statement generator" on the Dilbert Web site: www.dilbert.com.[6]

What's Your One-Liner?

For a vision to have impact, it must be simple and profound. How do you attain both? By keeping your vision to ten words or less. The folks at Sequoia Capital, the prominent venture firm behind such companies as Cisco, Google, and Apple, call it "the one-liner": a concise statement that tells people what you do. Condensing the statement, or vision, into ten words or less reflects your command of the business and your market. As one venture capitalist told me, "If you can't say it in ten words or less, I'm not investing, I'm not buying, I'm not coming on board, I'm not leasing you space. Period."

This sounds harsh, but the venture capitalist makes a good point. We all have audiences that we need to influence. Whether they are customers, employees, landlords, bankers, or investors, they want to "get it fast." They want to know whether your company, product, or service is worth exploring. We make immediate judgments about people all the time; do we want to do business with them, buy their product, lend them money, or join them as employees? In other words, do we want to be a part of their world? We make these judgments based on a person's ability to articulate a vision clearly and simply.

Imagine sitting in the offices of Sequoia Capital when two young college grads walked in and asked for money. Sergey Brin and Larry Page had no business experience and no track record in starting companies, but they offered something even more powerful: a one-line vision. Brin and Page told the venture capitalists, "We deliver the world's information in one click." That was it. The investors "got it" immediately and put their money behind a company called Google. That vision set the stage for a conversation that would change the way most of us get our information and would create billionaires of its founders.

When Sandy Lerner and Len Bosack walked into Sequoia Capital to seek investors for a new company called Cisco Systems, they could have said something like "Based on IP/TCP protocol, we build routers, switches, and hubs that will take data and blah, blah, blah." But instead they said three words: "We network networks." It was simple but profound, especially at the time when computers were linked to each other within intra-networks but the networks themselves had no way of talking to each other. With that one-liner, the partners at Sequoia got it immediately, funded Cisco, and the company went on to transform the way we use the Internet to live, work, play, and learn.

Doug Ducey was named CEO of Cold Stone Creamery in 2000 and set an ambitious goal: to grow from 74 franchise stores to 1,000 in five years. According to Ducey, crafting a compelling vision was critical to getting buy-in from the existing franchise community at the time.[7] The vision he delivered met the criteria of an inspiring one-liner: "The world will know us as the ultimate ice-cream experience." The statement Ducey crafted meets all the criteria of a powerful one-line vision. It is specific (ice cream), consistent (the line appears on the vision statement posted in all stores), and memorable. Ducey's one-liner harnessed the collective passion and talent of Cold Stone's existing community and served to attract new talent. Five years later, Cold Stone did meet its goal for 1,000 stores and is now ranked as the third largest ice-cream chain in the country. In May 2007, Cold Stone merged with Kahala to create a holding company for 13 brands. Ducey was named CEO of Kahala Cold Stone and now has the opportunity to inspire even more franchise owners with his remarkable ability to craft and deliver a powerful vision. (See Figure 2.1.)

Masters and Commanders: Examples of Inspiring Navigators

LIGHTS, HOPE, AND REVIVAL

J. Wayne Leonard is the chairman and CEO of Entergy, America's third largest energy company. He is also one of the most inspiring

Figure 2.1 Kahala Cold Stone CEO Doug Ducey scoops a giant serving of vision at an annual franchise conference.
Photo by W. Scott Mitchell, "Doug 2007 AFM 2," 2007. Photo courtesy of Cold Stone Creamery.

individuals I met during the research for this book. Entergy generates power for 2.6 million customers in half a dozen southern states. In August 2005, Hurricane Katrina knocked out electricity to more than 1 million Entergy customers. Approximately 1,500 Entergy employees were displaced, many of whom no longer had homes. One lineman and his friends were caught in the rising water. They fled to the attic of the man's home and used a two-by-four to bust through the roof. The next day, after being rescued, that lineman joined his fellow workers to turn the lights back on for Entergy's customers.

His story was not unusual. Crews worked sixteen-hour days for more than a week, while still unable to check their own homes. By the end of the first week, power was restored to over half a million customers, and nearly everyone got power back by the end of September—a remarkable achievement by all accounts. But what I find truly extraordinary is the fact that none of the affected employees *had* to return to work. They *wanted* to. They were told that their first duty was to take care of themselves and their families; they were told that their jobs would be there when they returned. The "when" was up to them. But for nearly every employee, the "when" was now!

Entergy's employees showed devotion, commitment, and a level of teamwork that should be the envy of corporate America. How did Entergy encourage such intense engagement by its employees? It starts at the top. Wayne Leonard is more than a boss. He considers his role as an inspiring leader to be the most important function of his office. Leonard has consistently cultivated a culture based on a simple mission: to leave this world a better place than how they found it. In other words, for Entergy employees, their work represents more than a paycheck.

"Our employees know that what they do makes a real difference in people's lives," Leonard told me during an interview for this book.[8] "We don't just provide electricity. We cool their homes in the summer and warm their homes in the winter. We allow people to cook their food, clean the environment, and educate their children. We do a lot more than make electricity and money." If Entergy's displaced employees had viewed their role as "just another job" instead of providing hope to those who lost their power, its customers might have remained in the dark a lot longer.

Entergy won numerous awards for its handling of the crisis, as did Leonard himself. It is easy to see why. Leonard wrote a string of emotional and optimistic email messages to all of his employees in the days and weeks after Katrina. I read more than two dozen of these emails. The correspondence reflects the power of a mission consistently and passionately conveyed. Here are some excerpts:

In every man and woman's life, there is a defining moment. It is a brief intersection of circumstances and choices that define a person for better or worse, a life of unfilled potential or a life that mattered, that made a difference. It is true of individuals and it is true of business. We have great passion for the difference we make in other's lives. We provide a commodity that sustains life. But, more importantly, we provide the most precious commodity of all—hope.

The task before us is awesome, but not insurmountable. We will be challenged at every turn, but this is what has always defined Entergy. We are at our best when the challenge is greatest.... Our response to this crisis will make the people we call Entergy remembered and revered for all time.... We are bruised but not broken. We are saddened but not despondent. We are at that remarkable place in time where hearts, minds and souls of the good cross with challenge and opportunity to set the course of history. We define ourselves here and now for all to see, everywhere.

Future generations will stand in awe at what you have endured and accomplished. Books will be written. Stories will be handed down. Some fall or spring day, the sun will be out, the temperature will be 70's and you'll be sitting on the front porch, content with the knowledge that you were not only there, but you stood tall and you didn't break or bend. Maybe it wasn't the life you envisioned, but in many ways it was better. Stronger, more courageous, more selfless than you ever even imagined you might be. You see things like this on television or in history books and ask "how did they do it?" Now, you can tell them because you did it. You were in the game. Maybe you were or maybe you weren't a "superstar" growing up. But I know this. You are now.[9]

Now wait a minute. Entergy provides electricity, doesn't it? Keeping the lights on—in and of itself—isn't inspiring. What the lights do to improve the lives of its customers is inspiring. The key to getting employees, customers, or clients fired up about your widget is not to sell the widget but to sell how the widget will improve their lives. We'll talk about this concept of selling the benefit more in the next chapter, but for now, can you imagine working for someone like Leonard—someone who speaks words of hope, optimism, and encouragement? Yes, Leonard is a remarkable leader. But so, too, do you have the ability to rally people to a better future and to bring out the best in others. What do you notice about the vision Leonard communicates? Entergy provides electricity. But in Leonard's world, the company and its employees create much more. They offer hope. Ordinary business professionals sell a product or service. But as the leader of your personal brand, you must offer much more—the promise of a better life for your customer, client, or employee. Peddle hope.

Many of your customers, colleagues, clients, or employees are tired, uninspired, and disillusioned precisely because they have no Leonard in their lives. J. Wayne Leonard is one of those rare individuals who understands that people will respond best when they know that their work is adding up to a great cause, bigger than themselves. It is up to you to communicate that vision. If not, how do you expect to get the best out of people? You can't and you won't. Entergy's employees believe in the power of their mission. In much the same way, the people in your sphere of influence will be inspired only if you navigate the way by crafting and delivering a bold vision they can believe in. It works for Leonard. It can work for you.

Unleash Dormant Forces

Here is an extraordinary description of the power of a compelling vision. It was written 2,000 years ago by Patanjali, the
founder of Yoga, but you do not have to contort your body into
bizarre positions to appreciate how profound it is: "When you
are inspired by some great purpose, some extraordinary project,
all your thoughts break their bonds, your mind transcends limitations, your consciousness expands in every direction, and you
find yourself in a new, great, and wonderful world. Dormant
forces, faculties, and talents become alive, and you discover yourself to be a greater person by far than you ever dreamed yourself
to be." Inspire others to some great purpose and watch as their
"dormant forces" come alive!

THE CORE PURPOSE BEHIND
THE STARBUCKS EXPERIENCE

In *Built to Last, Successful Habits of Visionary Companies*, authors
Jim Collins and Jerry Porras studied eighteen leading companies. The
research was substantial, but the conclusion was simple: Individuals
are inspired by "core values and a sense of purpose beyond just making
money."[10] Think of your one-line vision as your core purpose—the
fundamental reason behind the existence of your company, service,
or product. The core purpose, argue Collins and Porras, must remain
"fixed over time" to prove effective. That means the strategy might
change to accommodate changes in market conditions, but the fundamental vision must remain consistent.

In an interview for *Business 2.0*, Xerox CEO Anne Mulcahy said,
"More than forty years ago, our founder, Joe Wilson, spelled out a set of
core values that cover how we engage with employees and customers,
how we deliver value, and how we behave. Every decision I make is

aligned with those values."[11] A vision that changes as often as Lindsay Lohan switches nightclubs does no good for anyone. A compelling vision must be vivid, exciting, and consistent.

When I wrote my first book, I interviewed Starbucks chairman Howard Schultz. Prior to our discussion, I read Schultz's book, *Pour Your Heart into It*. Schultz is passionate about what he does; in fact, the word "passion" appears on nearly every page. But it soon becomes clear that he is not as passionate about the coffee as he is about the people, the Baristas who make the Starbucks experience what it is. You see, Schultz's core vision was not to build a coffee shop. It was much bigger and much more altruistic. His mission was to build a company that treats people with dignity and respect, a vision that has remained consistent, or fixed, over time. When I reviewed the transcripts from my time with Schultz, I was struck by the fact that the word "coffee" rarely appeared. Schultz's vision had little to do with making great coffee and everything to do with how happy employees offer exceptional customer service.

His vision is remarkably consistent. His book was written 10 years before our interview and yet his vision had not changed. One year later Schultz appeared on CNBC's *Big Idea with Donnie Deutsch* and articulated exactly the same vision:

Schultz: Starbucks is the quintessential experience brand and that brand is brought to life by our people. . . . we have no patent, no secret sauce whatsoever. . . . The only competitive advantage we have is the relationship we've built with our people and the relationship they have built with the customer.

Deutsch: You're talking about your competitive advantage but you haven't mentioned the word coffee.

Schultz: We're in the people business. Of course we sell coffee as a product, but we're in the people business. It's all human connection. We've been able to crack the code at creating

an environment where people are treated well, they're re-
spected, and they're valued. Customers come in and can
see it's a different kind of environment, almost an oasis.[12]

It is important to remember that Schultz was able to light a fire
in his own heart before igniting enthusiasm in others. In fact, a vivid
description of your vision is largely meaningless without mastering
Simple Secret #1 (Ignite Your Enthusiasm). Although the 7 Simple
Secrets are qualities shared by inspiring business professionals and
not "steps," the second trait is ineffective without the first. "Passion,
emotion, and conviction are essential parts of the vivid description,"
write Collins and Porras. "Some managers are uncomfortable with
expressing emotion about their dreams, but it's the passion and emotion
that will attract and motivate others."[13] Schultz is passionate about the
meaning his brand brings to the lives of his employees. He wears it on
his sleeve. It is part of his magic.

TELL ME THE SECRET TO YOUR SUCCESS

When is the last time you heard about employees giving their CEO
a standing ovation after a staff presentation? When have you heard
employees say their staff meetings are like going to church because
they make everyone feel good about the purpose of their organization?
Mike McCue elicits this type of reaction from his employees. (See
Figure 2.2.) McCue is the cofounder and CEO of Tellme Networks.
You may not have heard the name of his company, but there is a good
chance the company's service helped you buy a pizza or movie tickets.
Call 1-800-Dominos and you will be routed to a friendly automated
voice that helps you find a local pizza joint and to satisfy your craving
all without pressing a button. Tellme is behind that transaction. Call
1-800-Fandango to order movie tickets and an automated voice will

Figure 2.2 Tellme Cofounder and CEO Mike McCue crafted a vision that inspired employees, customers, and investors.
Photo by Ken Cook, "Mike McCue Photo," February 14, 2007. Photo courtesy of Tellme.

help you find show times and buy tickets. Tellme is behind that purchase. Call 1-800-GoFedEx and an automated voice menu will help you schedule a pickup or track a package. Tellme is behind that information. In fact, more than 40 million people a month use Tellme's network to find the information they need.

On March 14, 2007, Microsoft announced plans to acquire Tellme for an estimated $1 billion. Microsoft CEO Steve Ballmer has a lot in common with Mike McCue. Both articulate a simple but profound vision to inspire investors, employees, and customers. Microsoft's mantra hasn't changed since Bill Gates first persuaded Ballmer to put "a computer on every desk in every home." Neither has Mc-Cue's vision changed since he started the company in 1999: "Say what you want into any phone and get it." McCue's one-liner never changed.

I had interviewed McCue prior to the Microsoft purchase. The power of his vision and his charismatic communication style had proven to be a hit with employees, colleagues, and investors long before Microsoft took notice. Some employees at Tellme had followed McCue from one company to the next. Several had worked with Mc-Cue at the first company he founded, Paper Software, and joined him at Netscape, where he served as the search engine's VP of Technology. When Netscape was sold to America Online, they followed him again to Tellme. McCue is a big believer in crafting a clear and compelling vision and reinforcing that vision through meetings, pitches, and presentations. He uses skillful communications to navigate a course for the company's 320 employees—employees who will be part of Microsoft's business division by the time you read this.

The media has tried to place a label on Tellme's service since the company started in 1999. At various times Tellme's technology has been called Dialtone 2.0, a voice portal, or Web search on the telephone. But to employees, the vision is simple and has always been the same.

"How has that big vision—to say what you want into any phone and get it—play a role in inspiring your employees, customers and investors?" I asked McCue.

"Life is too short to do something small," he responded.[14] "There are two things that really matter to great people: They want to do something big with their lives and they want to learn from other great people. Those are two very powerful motivators."

Reinventing the way people and businesses use the telephone is a big vision, a massive mountain to climb. But McCue does not believe that employees can just put on their backpacks and scale the mountain.

He believes short-term goals have to be communicated and celebrated along the way.

To verbally reinforce the vision, McCue is fond of using a Mt. Everest analogy in his presentations. At one staff meeting, he showed a slide of Everest and graphically inserted "base camps" to visually represent the stages the company had conquered or had yet to reach. For example, answering 1-800 numbers for large corporations became "Base Camp 1." Camp 2 represents the goal of operating all directory assistance in the United States. (Tellme currently handles the mobile 411 calls on Cingular and Verizon.) Each camp is set up with an eye on the summit: Say what you want into any phone and get it.

"Camp 1 might have a lot of revenue attached to it, but that is not why the company got started," says McCue. "I try to motivate people to reach a particular camp and then connect the dots for them. Otherwise people might lose sight of the vision. The value I add to the company is to get people out of the warm, dry tents and sleeping bags for the march to the next camp." McCue is effective at keeping the eyes of his team trained on the summit, but he reminds them not to lose sight of the short-term goals as well. McCue believes it can be terribly demotivating to feel as if you are not making progress toward a big vision. When navigating the way, inspiring communicators keep their eyes on the summit but both feet on the ground.

It doesn't surprise me that Microsoft CEO Steve Ballmer would have been inspired by McCue. Ballmer owes his success at Microsoft to the power of a simple and consistent vision. During a speech at Stanford University in March 2007, Ballmer told the audience that six weeks after dropping out of Stanford to join Microsoft, he thought he had made a mistake. Bill Gates and his father took him out for drinks and said, "You don't get it. You said you just joined to become the bookkeeper of a 30-person company. But we're going to put a computer on every desk in every home."[15] According to Ballmer, that "mantra" stuck for seventeen years.

A Vision Turned Mantra

Everyone at Microsoft could repeat Gates's mantra—the one-liner to put a computer on every desk in every home. To Cranium founder Richard Tait, this edict reflected the power of a vision clearly and consistently communicated. Tait learned from that experience, taking the concept of a vision statement and turning it into much more—a calling, a movement, an opportunity to lighten and enlighten people's lives. The Cranium mantra is in the acronym CHIFF: Clever, High quality, Innovative, Friendly and Fun.[16] At first, all major product decisions were measured against these qualities, but soon employees began to apply CHIFF to everything. It is not uncommon to see a response in an email "Not CHIFF." CHIFF has become a common language, a way of communicating the vision of the company between Tait and his colleagues without having the company founder in the same room. Everyone measures success by asking "Is it CHIFF?" The philosophy permeates every aspect of the company, from employee orientations to staff meetings, press releases, marketing collateral, game design, or any one of hundreds of touch points where the standard is applied daily.

KODAK'S NEW IMAGE

Inspiring individuals use words rich in imagery to communicate their vision. The image of McCue leading his employees to the summit of Mt. Everest is simple, clear, exciting, and filled with rich imagery. But while McCue is scaling the summit, Kodak CEO Antonio Perez is burning the boats.

In 2000 Kodak committed itself to bolstering its declining film business by becoming a leader in digital cameras. Despite heavy skepticism in the business community, within five years Kodak had accomplished its goal to become the number-one seller of digital cameras. Along came Antonio M. Perez in 2003, who discovered that the new strategy was not working as well as planned. While camera sales had soared 40 percent to $5.7 billion, cameras were a low-margin business. Inexpensive competitors flooded the market, and easy-to-shoot cameras quickly became commodities.

As of this writing, Perez is attempting to reshape Kodak with a new strategy intended to capitalize on the demand to share and store photographs easily on a PC or online. His vision is simple: Help people organize and manage their library of personal images. According to *BusinessWeek*, when Perez was promoted to CEO, he called a meeting with his top executives and discussed the change in the company's vision, saying simply "You have to burn the boats."[17] The point he was making: There would be no turning back once the strategy was under way. It is too early to tell whether the initiative will turn around Kodak's fortunes, but if it fails, it will not be for lack of vision. Perez understands the need to communicate an energizing vision and to rally others behind it.

Perez is not alone in his quest to remake his company. In an IBM survey taken in March, 2006, 65 percent of the world's top CEOs said they plan on making radical changes to their companies in the next two years[18]—which is all the more reason to learn inspiring speaking techniques to convince employees and customers that the changes will benefit them and the company. Big changes require enthusiastic spokespeople and a compelling vision to get everyone on board.

WENDY KOPP GETS AN A FOR VISION

Reaching Teach for America (TFA) founder Wendy Kopp is far from easy. It is hard to hear her over the loudspeakers of an airline terminal, but I had to deal with it if I wanted to include her insights in this book. Seventeen years after starting the nonprofit, Kopp logs thousands of miles yearly, traveling three times a week to visit schools in impoverished areas who hire TFA members.

As a senior at Princeton, Kopp had a dream "to build a movement to eliminate educational inequities." That was her one-liner seventeen years ago and remains consistent today. The power of that vision kept her going despite the significant hurdles she had to overcome to raise the millions of dollars and to recruit the thousands of college students required to make the program successful.

Today TFA places college graduates for two-year stints at some of America's most troubled urban and rural schools. The program boasts of 12,000 alumni who have gone through the program. Forty-four hundred TFA members currently teach at 1,000 schools around the country. Nineteen thousand college seniors apply every year. TFA hires more college graduates than most Fortune 500 firms, more than Microsoft, Procter & Gamble, and General Electric. A full 10 percent of the senior class at Dartmouth and Yale opt for a two-year tour with TFA instead of accepting more lucrative positions in other professions. Kopp's vision is to have a direct impact on thousands of schoolchildren across the country.

According to Kopp, she set out on a vision most people thought was impossible.[19] But her passion and commitment to the goal ultimately allowed her to leap the hurdles to making her dream successful. Crafting a big, exciting vision is just as important for TFA members who are faced with enormous teaching challenges. "In the context in which we are working, our members must set a vision that most people would think is crazy and convince kids why it's important to accomplish that goal. It's fundamentally important. Let's say you're a fourth-grade teacher and your kids are operating at a first-grade level. The teacher who set a vision that most people think is crazy, like saying every one of those kids will pass the fourth-grade test before entering fifth grade, will have a greater chance of success and ultimately make a huge difference in the lives of those kids."

In November 2006 Wendy Kopp appeared on the cover of *Fortune* magazine. "What did that mean to you?" I asked. "I thought it would really help the cause," Kopp said. "It tells parents of college students that TFA will be good for their kids. It validates the cause for promising future leaders." Kopp isn't about ego. She's about vision. Kopp doesn't need to see herself on the cover of a national magazine to feel important, but if it helps "the cause," then it's good. Kopp will keep traveling, recruiting, and fundraising because her vision is not yet complete. But for the 19,000 members who have gone through the program, her vision opened up a world of change.

Big, Hairy, Audacious Goals

The *Built to Last* authors deserve credit for introducing a catchy term into the business lexicon: the big, hairy, audacious goal (BHAG). All companies have goals, "but there is a difference between merely having a goal and becoming committed to a huge, daunting challenge—like a big mountain to climb.... A true BHAG is clear and compelling and serves as a unifying focus point of effort—often creating immense team spirit."[20] According to Collins and Porras, a BHAG is engaging, hitting people right in the gut. It is tangible, energizing, and requires little or no explanation. A BHAG should not be reserved for companies. If you are serious about building your personal brand, about being inspired and inspiring, then your vision has to be worthy of following.

Who's in Your Mars Group?

A memorable vision takes off within an organization when a select group of colleagues, customers, or employees believes in the goal and becomes a group of evangelists, fervently spreading the vision to others.

The *Built to Last* authors call it the Mars Group: "Imagine you've been asked to re-create the very best attributes of your organization on another planet, but you only have seats on the rocket ship for five to seven people. Who would you send? They are the people who likely have a gut level understanding of your core values, have the highest level of credibility with their peers, and the highest level of competence."[21]

Perez does not call his idea the Mars Group, but it encompasses the same thing. According to *BusinessWeek*, Perez believes that in any organization, one-third of the staff will readily support change, one-third can be convinced, and one-third will be unwilling to make the change. "To help him win over a clear majority, he assembled a group of people who were skeptical by nature and assigned them to a committee he called the R Group ('R' stood for Rebels). He asked them to make suggestions on how the company could be improved. Once these people felt like they were part of the conversation for change, they spread the word throughout the organization that Perez was a good leader, and because they had credibility, their opinions influenced many others."[22] A major key to navigating the way is to develop a group of soldiers who march for your cause and rally the troops along the way. It takes teamwork to turn a vision into reality.

CONNECTING WITH TRAVELOCITY'S CEO

"Employees need to understand the vision, how it tangibly impacts them and how their job contributes to that vision," Travelocity CEO Michelle Peluso, told me.[23] "If they can't emotionally grasp on to something, then it's hard for them to be motivated. Secondly, senior leaders need to care about their staff. If employees know that you genuinely care about their well being and you create evangelists among the organization, it spreads like wildfire." Peluso gets it. She understands the value of articulating a Big, Hairy, Audacious Goal and creating a group of evangelists to spread the vision.

In the last ten years, Travelocity has gone from a simple Web site selling flights to the fifth largest travel agency in the United States, offering a range of flights, hotels, car rentals, vacation packages, show tickets, and more. "If you're genuine, passionate and have a clear vision, it resonates with your employees," says Peluso. She believes that energized employees will put in the extra effort required for success in today's fiercely competitive landscape. And for Travelocity, the extra effort involves improving on the customer experience. Satisfying the customer is everything for Travelocity. Unhappy customers will not return and, potentially more damaging, will tell the world about their unpleasant experience. Since Peluso cannot possibly have a personal relationship with the company's 5,000 employees worldwide, conveying the company's core vision becomes essential to its continued success. Having a clear vision gives everyone a road map to doing their jobs, whether Peluso is in the room or not.

Everyone at Travelocity internalizes the company's core ideology. The role of each employee is to champion a great travel experience for all Travelocity customers. That's the vision, and Peluso believes it is far more emotional than articulating a more limiting mission, such as "to have the best technology." Peluso's role is to make sure everyone, in every part of the organization, understands how their work relates to the vision she has set for the company. Employees are taught to ask "What does this mean to champion a customer experience in my job? What can I do to deliver a great experience?"

The person working on flight algorithms knows that being a customer champion means helping customers find better prices than Travelocity's competitors. The people loading hotel information understand that being a customer champion means finding the best hotels in a customer's price range. The employees soliciting customer reviews and writing content believe that being a customer champion means giving customers the most accurate, up-to-date information on their destinations. Peluso keeps the vision at top of mind as well. "Even if my job is crafting contracts with our suppliers, I need to make sure those contracts include fair terms and strong assurances that those suppliers are going to treat our customers well. Everything ties back to championing the customer experience."

Peluso reinforces the Travelocity vision by communicating constantly and consistently. Her techniques include:

- *Weekly emails to all staff.* The emails describe how they are delivering against their vision to champion the customer experience. In addition, employees are asked to nominate a colleague whom they believe reflects the company's core values. Peluso features the nominees in her weekly emails along with detailed descriptions of how their service ties back to the mission.
- *Monthly brown-bag lunches that anyone can attend.* These lunches are energizing and lively and invite open and honest discussion.
- *Quarterly visits to the global office.* There Peluso discusses the company's financial status and how the company can continue to improve its position among its competitors.

Like all of the inspiring individuals featured in this book, Peluso believes that people are motivated by more than a paycheck. Providing a salary and benefits are the cost of entry to attracting great people. Today more than ever, employees want to work for someone whose vision represents a grander purpose. People "internalize compensation" for a few hours or days, says Peluso.

But it doesn't fire people up to get out of bed every morning, unless of course it's bonus day! Seriously, you don't get up saying, I've got great compensation. You go to work because you believe in the people around you, your peers, your colleagues, and when you believe your company does something great for your customers. You're proud to handle a customer call or supplier meeting to discuss Travelocity. You need to feel as though you're learning, growing, stretching yourself and you think you work with cool people—people with integrity, who are smart, have a sense of fun, hold each other accountable and expect great things from each other. When you get it right, the whole thing comes together nicely.

For Peluso, it has come together nicely. Her enthusiasm, skill, and vision have all come together to create an exceptional work environment for her employees and a better travel experience for her customers.

A Lesson from the Richest Man Who Ever Lived

To Solomon, a vision was not abstract at all. For him, gaining a true vision was more like using a highway atlas. It means having a perfectly clear picture of an ultimate destination and a detailed road map to get there.

—Steven K. Scott, The Richest Man Who Ever Lived [24]

Frame the Vision around a Grand Purpose

Everything starts with a vision: finding a new job, motivating a team before the big game, or creating a successful sales presentation. We all have vision, and we apply that vision every day in some capacity. You would not get out of bed in the morning unless you had a vision to accomplish something, even if it is just making a pot of coffee. The difference between average communicators and inspiring individuals is the fact that the latter frame their vision around a grand purpose that can be expressed simply. Here are examples of grand visions that have changed the course of humanity, each of which was met with skepticism when it was first introduced:

- "We will build a motor car for the great multitude. It will be large enough for the family but small enough for the individual to run and care for. It will be constructed of the best materials, by the best men to be hired, after the simplest designs that modern engineering can devise. But it will be so low in price that no man making a good salary will be unable to own one and enjoy the blessing of hours of pleasure in God's great open spaces."

  —Henry Ford, 1907

- "I believe that this nation should commit itself to achieving the goal, before this decade is out, of landing a man on the moon and returning him safely to the earth. No single space project in this period will be more impressive to mankind, or more important for the long-range exploration of space."

  —John F. Kennedy at a joint session of Congress on May 25, 1961

- "We in the West stand ready to cooperate with the East to promote true openness, to break down barriers that separate people, to create a safe, freer world. And surely there is no better place than Berlin, the meeting place of East and West, to make a start. Let us use this occasion, the 750th anniversary of this city, to usher in a new era, to seek a still fuller, richer life for the Berlin of the future.... General Secretary Gorbachev, if you seek peace, if you seek prosperity for the Soviet Union and Eastern Europe, if you seek liberalization: Come here to this gate! Mr. Gorbachev, open this gate! Mr. Gorbachev, tear down this wall!"

  —Ronald Reagan at the Brandenburg Gate, June 12, 1987 [25]

WHAT DREAMS ARE MADE OF

In Chapter 4 you will learn much more about rhetorical devices to wow your listeners. But for now, keep in mind that the successful articulation of a vision requires language that is both rich in imagery and devoid of weak, empty, and ambiguous words. Persuasive speakers have long understood the power of imagery to stir emotions—the creation of mental pictures through the words they use. Framing mental pictures as "dreams" is a rhetorical technique used by the most charismatic leaders of our time. They use the technique because it works.

On the step of the Lincoln Memorial on August 28, 1963, Martin Luther King Jr. expressed his vision of racial harmony:

> I have a dream that one day on the red hills of Georgia the sons of former slaves and the sons of former slave owners will be able to sit down together at the table of brotherhood. I have a dream that one day even the state of Mississippi, a desert state sweltering with the heat of injustice and oppression, will be transformed into an oasis of freedom and justice. I have a dream that my four little children will one day live in a nation where they will not be judged by the color of their skin but by the content of their character. I have a dream today.

Los Angeles Mayor Antonio Villaraigosa, the first Hispanic mayor elected in that city since 1872, vividly expressed his vision during his inauguration remarks on July 1, 2005:

> I am asking you to dream with me. Dream with me of a Los Angeles where our kids can walk to school in safety and where they receive an education that gives them a genuine opportunity to pursue their own dreams. Dream with me of a Los Angeles that's the leading economic and cultural center in the world. As Venice was in the 15th century, as London was in the 19th century, Los Angeles can and will be the great

global city of our century. Dream with me of a Los Angeles where it doesn't matter whether you're African American, Latino, Caucasian, or Asian. Whether you're Jewish or Muslim, Protestant or Catholic. Whether you're from Watts or Westwood. Where every Angeleno is an equal stakeholder in our city's future. Angelenos, we need to start thinking big again, and facing up to our biggest challenges. I intend to be a mayor who confronts those challenges. And I'll begin by leading the fight to making our neighborhoods safer.[26]

In speaking to students at Tsinghua University in Beijing on November 15, 2005, Arnold Schwarzenegger asked the audience to share his dreams: "I want to talk to you about dreams, because I am an expert in dreams. . . . America believes in the power of the individual and what the individual can accomplish. Imagine what could be accomplished if the dreams of 1.3 billion individuals could be unleashed."[27]

Illinois senator Barack Obama catapulted to the national stage after delivering a keynote speech at the 2004 Democratic National Convention, a speech in which he professed: "I stand here today, grateful for the diversity of my heritage, aware that my parents' dreams live on in my two precious daughters. I stand here knowing that my story is part of the larger American story, that I owe a debt to all of those who came before me, and that, in no other country on earth, is my story even possible."[28]

I include these examples of dream imagery to demonstrate the fact that clear and effective communication of a vision must contain image-rich words that paint a vivid picture of the future in the minds of listeners. No, I do not expect you to use the word "dream" in your next presentation—unless it is appropriate. But pay careful attention to the words you use, especially when articulating your vision. Your words must help your listeners form a mental picture of where you plan to take them.

> **Everyone Needs Vision**
>
> Cordell Parvin is a Dallas attorney who coaches young lawyers. Vision, he says, is one of the keys to becoming a successful lawyer. "A law firm leader must be able to express his or her vision for the firm in a way that creates excitement in the firm. Almost nothing energizes people more than feeling they are a part of building something special.... obviously a law firm vision is not as dramatic as going to the moon or overcoming prejudice, but the firm leader can convey a sense of hope, opportunity and a 'can-do' spirit to lawyers and staff."[29]

SURVIVING THE SALES PITCH

In addition to using words rich in imagery, inspiring speakers avoid weak language that suck the life and energy out of those images. When Mark Burnett pitched the concept of *Survivor* to CBS, the key to his success was articulating a bold, captivating vision. Burnett told *Selling Power* magazine that he walked into CBS with a mock copy of *Newsweek* showing *Survivor* on the cover. "That's how big this is going to be," he told the studio suits.[30] What an attention grabber!

"All success begins with the ability to sell something, whether it's a shirt or an idea," Burnett said.[31] Burnett is a masterful salesman. He takes a calculating approach to sales, whether he is selling T-shirts on Venice Beach (his first experience of American capitalism) or parlaying his love for competition into reality shows like *Survivor* and *The Apprentice*. One of Burnett's strategies is to pay careful attention to the person he is pitching to and to alter his approach based on how he reads the prospect. For example, Burnett says an analytical person wants more information, so he will barrage the listener with facts and statistics. An emotional person might be more interested in how something looks and sounds. But one thing is constant: Burnett always has a big vision of endless possibilities, and he frames that vision in words that reflect his enthusiasm and confidence in the project.

Fans of NBC's *The Apprentice* have Burnett's skills of persuasion to thank. Donald Trump's agent originally turned down the idea. Burnett, undeterred, visited Trump directly and won over the mega-mogul. By his own admission, Burnett found Trump to be intimidating, but he delivered a clear, concise, and energetic pitch. In the introduction to Burnett's book, *Jump In!* Trump writes, "Mark is a great leader as well as a visionary—an unbeatable combination for out-of-the-box success.... Mark was able to describe an exciting, incredible, groundbreaking show to me because he could already see it happening. He convinced me to see it his way, and because of his vision we've got a huge hit on our hands."[32] Of course I was not in the room when Burnett made his pitch, but I think it is safe to say Trump would have thrown him out if the conversation had gone something like this:

Trump: What makes you think this new show of yours will be a hit?
Burnett: Well, you know, it might be. We think it might be successful based on, uh, you know, our experience with other shows that have done okay. Look, you should have received the treatment. What do you think? Do you like it? If it's not what you expected, I'm sorry. We can, you know, uh, work on it.

Burnett certainly does not speak this way; neither do any of the inspiring invididuals featured in this book. Successful sales pitches require a compelling vision rich in imagery and devoid of weasel words, qualifiers, fillers, or ambiguous language. Here are some words and phrases that should rarely make their way into your communications and *never* have a place in your vision or one-liner:

- Maybe
- I think
- Well, you know
- Kinda
- Sorta
- I'm sorry; what I'm trying to say is . . .
- Uh, Um, Ah, and other types of filler words
- Buzzwords of any type (e.g., mission-critical, optimized, or monetize)

You don't have to eradicate each and every occurrence of these words or phrases in your speech. But it is similar to a doctor recommending one glass of red wine to lower your risk of heart disease. Medical professionals rarely make such recommendations because they know that one glass can easily become three, four, or five glasses, effectively destroying any health benefits that could have come from sticking to one glass a day. If you give yourself the green light to use filler words, you might go overboard. Instead, try to avoid these words completely so you have room to stumble now and again.

Buzzwords that Kill

Some words are simply empty, meaningless, trite, and overused. Venture capitalist Michael Mortiz, a partner with Sequoia Capital and one of the early investors in Google, once told *Business 2.0*, "The only thing that leaves me cold during a pitch from a startup is the use of drop-dead words or phrases: 'synergy,' 'no-brainer,' and 'slam dunk.'"[33] For a complete list of dreaded buzzwords, visit www.buzzwhack.com.

Inspiring individuals are drawn to their vision of a brighter future and, in as Marcus Buckingham says, have the ability to rally people to the better future they see. It is the power of your words that will ultimately feed your audience's imagination and encourage them to back your vision and values. If you can articulate a compelling vision of the world that is specific, consistent, and memorable, you will not only have grabbed their attention, but you will have captured their hearts. And where their hearts lead, their minds are sure to follow.

CHAPTER 3

Sell the Benefit

Put Your Listeners First

Positioning is about what you do for your customers—not
about what you want to become.

— Guy Kawasaki

Venture capitalists are a tough audience, which is why I often turn
to them for insight into what makes a persuasive pitch or presentation. Successful investors look for several qualities in entrepreneurs,
including enthusiasm and vision, which we discussed in the previous
chapters. But while those qualities are the price of admission to the
inner circle, they are not enough. Enthusiasm energizes and vision
inspires, but *focus* persuades. Focused entrepreneurs know their target
market and can clearly explain how their product or service improves
the lives of people and businesses in that market. Being able to describe
the benefit in crisp, clear, and compelling language tells a potential
investor that an entrepreneur is focused on what the product can do for
customers, which is where every entrepreneur's attention should be.
The lobbies of venture capital firms from New York to Silicon Valley
are littered with the dashed dreams of would-be entrepreneurs who

were enthusiastic and had a bold vision but failed to inspire investors. The most captivating entrepreneurs—those who walk out with a wad of cash and a chance to change the world—succeed by mastering Simple Secret #3: They sell the benefits.

People are inspired when they know how your product or service will improve their lives. You might never be in a position to ask a venture capital firm for money, but you pitch your company, service, or vision all the time: in every sales presentation, fundraising speech, job interview, or staff meeting. Every time you try to attract a customer, an employee, a partner, an investor, or a service provider, the person on the other end of the conversation is asking herself whether she wants to be part of your business or run the other way. Make no mistake: When you speak, your listeners are asking themselves one question: *What's in it for me?* It's the one question that should be answered not once, but throughout your communication. By answering this one question—*What's in it for me?*—you will stand apart from your competitors, inspire your clients, and enjoy far more success than you ever imagined.

"I'm a Mac and I'm a PC"

In 2006 Apple launched a memorable ad campaign called "I'm a Mac and I'm a PC." You must have seen one of the ads. In the television spots, a young, trendy-looking guy plays the Mac while the other frumpy and disheveled character actor plays the PC. In one ad the conversation goes like this:

Mac: Hello, I'm a Mac.
PC: And I'm a PC.
Mac: What happened to you? *The Mac turns toward the PC.*
PC: Kids happened. I was bought for a home and now I have to make movies and blogs and listen to music. You were made to

stimulate ten year old brains with your "iLife" jazz while all I want to do is balance their checkbooks.

Mac: I don't think ten-year-olds have checkbooks.

PC: No checkbooks, no inboxes, no employers; just wild imaginations.[1]

The ads are very funny and drive home the key point of this chapter. Apple inspires customers by focusing its marketing efforts on selling the benefits behind its products. The TV spots are carried on the company's Web site along with 15 reasons "Why You'll Love a Mac." The list contains no features, just *benefits*.[2] For example:

> #2: You can make amazing stuff.
> #10: More fun with photos.
> #11: Hollywood-style movies.
> #15: Awesome out of the box.

A client once asked me, "How can I be more like Steve Jobs in my next presentation?"

"It's simple," I explained to him. "Tell your listeners why you're excited about your product [Simple Secret #1], share a vivid vision of the future that your product makes possible [Simple Secret #2], and be specific about how your product will help them succeed in business [Simple Secret #3]."

Most people hype features. Steve Jobs sells benefits. When he pitches products, it's not about him; it's about you. That is the secret behind a master showman.

The Mom Test

Entrepreneur Mike McCue, the founder of Tellme Networks, uses his mom as a measure of success. He calls it, simply enough, the "Mom Test." If he can explain a product to his mother that makes her (a) understand it and (b) want to use it, then he knows he has got a winner.[3]

Do More with Dual Core

Picture this for a moment: You walk into a large consumer electronics store to shop for a new computer. A clerk in a bright blue shirt approaches you and asks some questions. Here are two scenarios for how the interaction might play out:

Scenario 1

Clerk:	How can I help you?
You:	I'm looking for a notebook computer. Mine is old, slow, and bulky.
Clerk:	Have you considered an Intel dual-core notebook?
You:	I've heard of Intel but not about "dual-core." Does Intel make notebooks?
Clerk (*dismissively*):	Of course not. Dual core processors have two full execution cores on a single micro-processor.
You (*eyes glazing over*):	Oh. Can you tell me more?
Clerk:	On a dual-core computer chip, there are two performance engines that can take more data and simultaneously process the data into rich multimedia content at a faster rate.
You (*more confused than ever*):	Okay. I don't think that's for me. Can you show me something else?

Unfortunately, this scenario is all too common and results in unsatisfied customers and lost sales. Let's try it again, this time with a salesperson who sells the benefits instead of touting the features.

Scenario 2

Eager Salesperson:	Good morning, can I help you look for something?
You:	Yes, I'm shopping for a new notebook computer. Mine is old, slow, and bulky.
Eager Salesperson:	They have come a long way. We have a wide selection of amazing computers that are light, small, and blazingly fast. Best of all, they won't break the bank. Will this be primarily for business or home?
You:	I'm looking for something light for business travel. But I also have a music library and enjoy watching DVDs on the airplane, something that has become very painful on my existing computer. The whole thing freezes up and everything crashes! It's very frustrating.
Eager Salesperson:	I understand. We'll find you one with a DVD player and you'll still be amazed at how small and light it is. I'm very excited about a new technology that hit the market. It's called Intel dual core. Have you heard of it?
You:	No, but I know about Intel. Do they make notebook computers now?
Eager Salesperson:	Intel does not manufacture computers, but it builds the microprocessor, "the brain," inside most computers. The advances Intel has made in chip design now allow the computer to make your life better, more enjoyable, and more productive than ever. Think of the microprocessor as one "brain" allowing your computer to function. New "dual-core" processors from Intel have

two brains instead of one. That means one brain can be working on one function while the other is doing something else. It's like having a sous-chef preparing the ingredients while the chef is cooking the meal. Two brains in one computer allow you do a lot of fun and productive things at the same time. For example, have you ever tried to download music from iTunes while your computer is running a virus scan in the background?

You: No way! My computer would crash!

Eager Salesperson: Not with a dual-core computer. In fact, you can download songs, send your friends an instant message, surf the Web, and run a comprehensive virus scan all at the same time. Here's the best part: You can do all that without seeing a decline in performance!

You (*laughing*):   Wow. That's neat. I don't think I'll ever multitask to that extent, but I get the idea.

Eager Salesperson: The power you get today in a small package really is amazing. I'm so glad I could share this information with you. You mentioned movies. Have you ever tried video editing? Do you record and capture home movies?

You: I've thought about it, but I'm afraid my current system will make the whole process just too frustrating.

Eager Salesperson: Dual-core chips make video editing a breeze.

You: Well there's no question in my mind that I should buy a computer with one of these Intel dual-core chips you've been telling me about. Can I see some models?

Eager Salesperson:	You bet. Let's have some fun. Once you experience it, you'll never go back. Here's a new system from Hewlett Packard....

It doesn't take a genius to figure out that the second scenario has a much better chance of leading to a sale. The first scenario is a sure-fire way to push a customer toward the door! We can learn three lessons from the second scenario—lessons that will help you define your value by focusing on your listener:

1. *Set up the problem before offering the solution.* The clerk in the first scenario assumes that you, the customer, recognize the benefit of a computer with "two performance engines." One common problem that prevents speakers from connecting with listeners is that they assume too much knowledge on the part of their audience. Outside the walls of your company, few people know how your product or service directly improves their lives. Help them to see the benefit immediately by describing a problem and setting the stage for your solution. The salesperson in the second scenario says that these new computers will make your life better, more enjoyable, and more productive than ever, and then proceeds to describe exactly how.

2. *Say it simply.* In the second scenario, the salesperson doesn't use technical jargon—phrases like "performance engine" and "simultaneous processing of information." Instead, the microprocessor is described as a "brain"—a visual analogy most people can understand. Every industry has jargon, or buzzwords, that few people outside of that particular industry recognize. Eliminating any words that are not common language for your audience is a necessary step to making your message easy to follow. Please keep in mind that I am not recommending that you eliminate all jargon and technical definitions from all your

communications. It is entirely acceptable if your listeners *ex-pect* it. But your message must be relevant to the people you are trying to reach. The first definition of dual core is perfectly appropriate for engineers but not for the average customer shopping for a new computer at her local Best Buy. Take the second approach and tailor your message for your audience.

3. *Use tangible, real-world examples.* Examples bring products or services to life and make them relevant to the lives of your listeners. It becomes easier for listeners to follow your message, and to take the action you desire, if they can see how the product fits into their lives. The first definition contains no specific example, just a confusing explanation about how dual-core chips process data at a faster rate. The second scenario is chock full of real-world examples—downloading songs from iTunes, instant messaging friends, running virus scans, or surfing the Web—all activities customers either have participated in or understand. These two words will do wonders for your communication: "For example." Use examples to pitch a product, service, or cause. The more complex your offering is, the more examples and case studies are required to motivate your listeners.

A Bridge over Geeky Waters

When Intel launched its first dual-core microprocessors in 2005, the company changed the way it conveys the message behind its technology. It replaced its traditional focus on "clock speed" and highly technical explanations of its products with a human face. But how do you put a human face on a computer component that most people never see? You accomplish this by selling the benefit.

Intel's television, print, retail, and outdoor marketing campaigns began promoting the benefits of the company's technology. Gone was the focus on product features alone. Instead, consumers saw people like themselves. For example, nothing will turn your brain to mush faster than a technical description of Intel's Xeon processor for servers. (A server is a powerful computer that sends data to other computers over an internal corporate network or via the Internet.) There are two ways of communicating the technology. You can use a technical definition: "Intel's Dual-Core Xeon processor provides scalable performance, robust virtualizations capabilities, and reliable uptime for demanding 64-bit enterprise applications."[4] This description is technically accurate and packed with product features, but it fails the inspiration test. Intel solved the problem with advertisements that featured people. In one ad, a doctor is standing behind a little girl in a hospital's new pediatric center. What does this have to do with Intel's Xeon-based processor server? The ad explains that the clinic was created out of what used to be a storage area. The 10,000-square-foot facility in a Thailand hospital was made possible because the hospital began using Intel-based servers to reduce its paper and documents. By getting rid of stored paper, the hospital freed up floor space and converted the area to a unit for sick children.[5] This example is touching, emotional, and defines Intel's value by focusing on what the technology means to people.

The goal of Intel's new advertising and marketing campaign was to generate excitement among a broader audience of customers. Intel spokespeople also began to change the way they talked about the technology. They added human elements—case studies and real-world examples—to their conversations, presentations, and interviews. Intel engineers and product managers have no problem talking technology. They can talk features all day long. Walk into an Intel conference room on any given day and you will find complicated mathematical

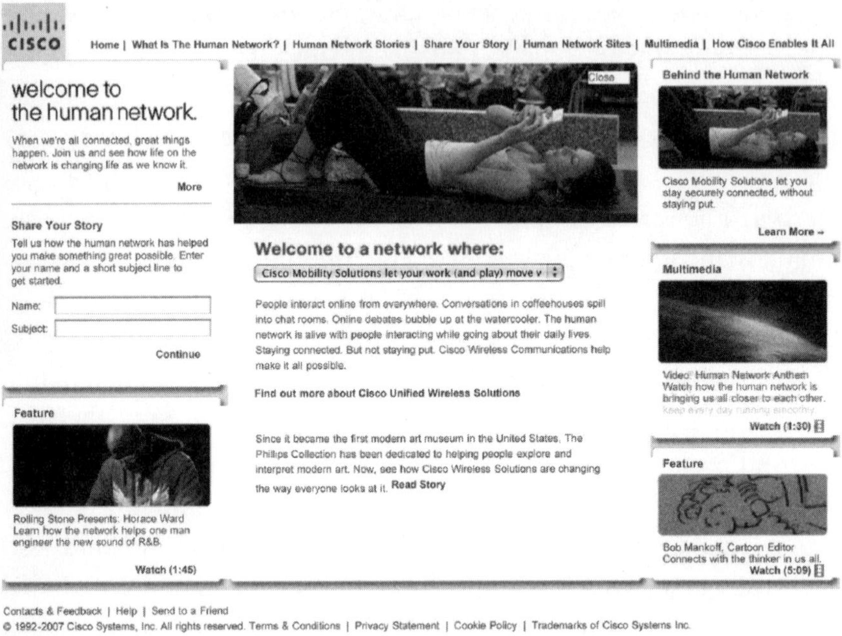

Figure 3.1 Cisco makes routers but sells human connection. (Image of woman from Cisco's Web site:
www.cisco.com/web/thehumannetwork/index.html.
Photo courtesy of Cisco Systems, Inc. Unauthorized use not permitted.

algorithms on whiteboards. But most customers outside of the company want to be inspired. Jargon and features do not inspire; people do. And people want to know what is in it for them.

The Human Network

In 2006 Cisco Systems launched a $100 million marketing campaign to put a human face on its networking gear. Cisco makes routers and switches—equipment that directs traffic over the Internet. Metal racks of equipment that most of us never see are not very inspiring, so Cisco featured stories about how the Internet was fundamentally changing the way we live, work, play, and learn. Cisco posted stories submitted by real people on its Web site, featured them in television and billboard advertisements, and also used them in executive presentations. (See Figure 3.1.)

The stories show how the Internet benefits real people by bringing them together, connecting people with each other—the Human Network. One story is about a mother whose son, Max, had been suffering from a rare respiratory virus. Doctors were stumped. But once the mother posted her story online, she connected with another woman whose child had the same affliction. They shared information and, within a month, Max was back to normal.[6] Today dozens of such stories are posted on Cisco's Web site along with links to resources demonstrating how the "human network" is bringing us all closer together. This human network campaign also finds its way into the language and presentations of Cisco executives and salespeople when they speak to customers, investors, or the media.

Like Intel, Cisco has learned that selling the human benefits of a product is far more inspiring than touting its features. Put a human face on features and you will hit a home run with your listeners.

Sell It Fast

In most professional conversations, you have all of one minute to grab someone's attention. Within a few seconds of meeting you, your listeners are already asking themselves "What's in it for me?" In *The Art of the Start*, former Apple evangelist turned venture capitalist Guy Kawasaki says, "Unfortunately, many entrepreneurs still believe that a pitch is a narrative whose opening chapter must always be autobiographical.... think again. It

(continued)

works in the opposite way: First, establish what you do.... Clear the air at the start of your pitch, and don't let anyone have to guess what you do. Make it short and sweet."[7]

Kawasaki makes a good point. All I would add is that when you establish what you do, what you do for the benefit of the individual listener is what matters. You might sell dog food. But if you sell dog food that tastes good and will let Rover live a longer life, then you've hooked me. It's not what you do for *yourself* that inspires me; it's what you do for me that motivates me to take action.

Learning Styles

At this point, you are probably coming up with creative ways to captivate your listeners the very next time you have an opportunity. During this preparation stage, let me give you one more thing to think about. It is commonly known that individuals generally fall into one of three learning styles: visual, auditory, or kinesthetic. Since it is difficult to discern learning patterns before communication takes place, especially with people whom you have never met, offering something for everyone will help you win over an individual or a room full of prospects.

FOR VISUAL LEARNERS

About 40 percent of us are visual learners. Creating a presentation loaded with images like photos, graphics, movies, and multimedia will go a long way toward helping your audience absorb the information. Remember, individuals are more likely to act on information they have a connection with, but they cannot connect with anything that they have not internalized. Visual learners connect through seeing.

Executives at flash memory maker SanDisk taught me a great deal about appealing to visual learners. Flash memory is a complicated technology, and SanDisk is full of engineers who could easily focus on technological features without making the content visual. But that would fail to generate excitement over their products, especially among consumers who buy their memory cards at retail. Without SanDisk flash memory cards, digital cameras would be pretty much useless. The company sells more than 100 million of these cards a year and has an annual revenue of over $2 billion. SanDisk has expanded well beyond digital cameras and now makes memory cards for all kinds of devices, including cell phones and portable game systems. SanDisk also makes the world's second-best-selling MP3 music and video player, the Sansa. Coming in second to the iPod is nothing to complain about!

The standard definition of "flash memory" is not very visual. According to Wikipedia, "Flash memory is a form of non-volatile computer memory that can be electrically erased and reprogrammed."[8] Not very exciting, is it? Instead, CEO Eli Harari and the other executives at SanDisk draw attention to what their products mean to the lives of their customers.[9] Here's how.

1. *Presentations are multimedia events.* Before executives say a word, SanDisk presentations kick off with thumping music, cool graphics, and movies of people enjoying the entire range of San-Disk products. The slides that follow contain stunning graphics. Where most companies would fill slides with text, SanDisk slides are full of colorful photos of the company's products. Words don't tell the SanDisk story. Products do, and products are visual.

2. *Executives show off products.* Catch any of the top executives on CNBC or Bloomberg television, and you'll often see them talking about products while holding up a cool new device. Seeing a gadget that stores thirty-three hours of video or 2,000 songs is

far more persuasive than simply talking about it. Seeing a flash memory card for your cell phone that stores 2,000 photographs and is no larger than the fingernail on your pinky makes a much stronger impact than a verbal description.

3. *Paint verbal pictures.* The words executives use paint a vivid picture of what SanDisk products mean to the lives of their listeners. For example, you might hear something like this: "Consumer devices like digital cameras, phones, and MP3 players are allowing people to stay connected and to share their most precious memories and digital entertainment with friends and family. SanDisk is at the heart of this trend. Our products let you store your music, pictures, and video, share them, and take them with you wherever you go. SanDisk is a leader in the industry. What does this mean to you? Walk into a Wal-Mart, Costco, or any of 200,000 retail stores in the world and you'll find our products." This description conjures word pictures in my mind's eye. I can see a digital camera, cell phone, and MP3 player storing photos, music, and video. I can see a SanDisk display at Costco or Wal-Mart. By painting word pictures, physically showing products, and using highly graphical images on their presentations, SanDisk spokespeople make the company tangible and exciting for visual learners.

FOR AUDITORY LEARNERS

Auditory learners, who represent about 20 to 30 percent of your audience, learn through listening. People who learn through listening benefit from some of the rhetorical techniques that are featured in Chapter 4, such as personal stories, metaphors, and analogies, but they also respond positively to a captivating voice, which can be an important weapon in your arsenal. I devoted about one-third of my previous book, *10 Simple Secrets of the World's Greatest Business*

Communicators, to the way great presenters talk, walk, and look. While I do not want to spend too much time on vocal delivery in this section, there are three techniques you can implement today to improve the way you sound:

1. *Vary the speed at which you speak.* Mesmerizing speakers will speed up and slow down during the course of their conversation. Presentations, especially, should have an ebb and flow. So should your delivery.
2. *Vary your tone.* Great speakers have inflections in their voice. Nothing lulls a listener to sleep faster than a speaker who talks in a monotone, with no variation in pitch.
3. *Pause for emphasis.* Right before you make a key point, pause for a second or two, and then deliver it.

FOR KINESTHETIC LEARNERS

Kinesthetic learners learn by doing, moving, and touching. In short, they are hands-on. They get bored listening for long periods of time. So include activities in your presentation to keep them engaged. If the group is small enough, get them to write down their ideas, or develop a part of the presentation that lends itself to note-taking. Demonstrations are also great for kinesthetic learners. I worked with one spokesperson for Clorox before the launch of a brand-new type of bleach that you can pour directly on clothes. Harold Baker is a Clorox scientist, but since he can tell you how to treat any kind of stain, he has affectionately become known as Dr. Laundry. Not only does he have his own Internet blog to help consumers solve their stain problems, he is also a popular radio and newspaper interviewee. He makes laundry fun (if that's possible).

When I was helping Doc Laundry rehearse for a round of media interviews, he decided to bring along a basket of sheets, towels, and other whites that had been washed with the new Clorox Ultimate Care bleach. Another basket had items washed in traditional bleach. When editors could feel how much softer the Ultimate Care clothes were and how much better they smelled, they were sold. Dr. Laundry had found the right prescription to win over his listeners!

You have no chance of persuading an individual if you don't sell the benefit of the message. But you can tell the "benefit" story much more effectively by addressing the needs of all three types of learners. All learners are bombarded by new forms of media: podcasts, computer games, ninety-second video clips on YouTube... The way you reach your audience must change along with the way people get their content. Keep all of these elements in mind. If you do not present your story in a way that is compelling to see, hear, and touch, it will be lost in the maze of media people now consume.

Don't Go Gettin' All High-Falutin'

While covering the 2000 presidential election, NBC's political analyst Tim Russert chose to avoid the computer-generated graphics the network made available and instead tallied the votes for viewers using a marker and a whiteboard. When it came time to predict which state would win the election, he simply grabbed the marker and wrote: "Florida, Florida, Florida."

Russert values simplicity, a quality he learned from his dad. His dad would say, "Don't get caught up in high-falutin' Washington talk. People want to know what's important and *why* it is important," Russert explained in an interview for *American Profile* magazine.[10]

My, What a Hard Drive You Have!

Every January about 150,000 people attend the world's largest consumer electronics show (known simply as CES). It used to be a fad-fest for gadget geeks but has turned into much more, with major movie and music producers using the platform to launch digital projects, such as movies and television shows on iPods. Journalists who cover the show are bombarded before they even hit the convention center with marketing material touting the latest and greatest innovation that will change the course of humankind (or at least allow you to control your TV, stereo, and computer without leaving your La-Z-Boy). It's up to journalists to make sense of it for their viewers and listeners.

Following the coverage of CES is a great lesson in selling the benefits. In January 2007 Seagate, the world's top maker of hard drives, launched products to make it easier for home PC users to back up the growing amount of digital files that take up a lot of space: movies, music, and photographs. The personal media servers Seagate was promoting made it possible to store those files, protect them, and access them from anywhere. Seagate, however, faced a challenge: Hard drives are not exciting. When was the last time you were inspired by the idea of magnetic surfaces on rotating platters inside your computer system? Seagate's goal was to pull a Justin Timberlake and bring the "sexy back." Company spokespeople succeeded in generating excitement among the press, analysts, and customers by selling the benefits. Jim Druckrey, senior vice president of Seagate's consumer products division, was quoted as saying "People don't care about the hardware, but they have a lot of emotional attachment to their content."[11] In its presentations and marketing materials for CES, Seagate reinforced that emotional connection by "selling" protection of your most cherished memories: the photographs, music, video, and business documents on your computer. Seagate could have easily touted the features of its portable hard drive: 160 gigabytes of storage, connects via USB 2.0 port, and carries a one-year warranty. Instead the company focused on the listener—customers—and what they valued—preserving their music, photos of their high school graduation, videos of their family vacations, and such. Seagate protects your digital life. Now, that is inspiring!

It's Not about You. It's about Them.

The amount of money companies spend on their CES presentations is staggering. Costs for the promotional video, slide development, and customized lighting can range from $80,000 to $100,000 and higher—and that's what second-tier companies spend! Major company keynotes can run much more. I know because I work with some corporate leaders who give keynote presentations at the conference. Since listeners make up their minds quickly, we tend to focus on kicking off the presentation with a bang. All too often, however, speakers begin with a slide titled "About Us." That would be fine, *if* the audience actually cared. I recommend to most clients that they do away with the "About Us" slide at the beginning of a presentation. Your listeners do not care about you. They care about what you can do for them. If you fail to tell your listeners how products or services benefit them, you'll lose their attention. If your product is going to change the world, advance an industry, or improve lives, hit me over the head with it right out of the gate.

Apple CEO Steve Jobs is a master at selling the benefit immediately. Jobs kicked off an October 2005 presentation in San Jose, California, by announcing that he has some "amazing" stuff to show the audience and that, like any good story, the presentation would be divided into three acts. He kicked off each "act" with new products, including the unveiling of the first video iPod. With each product, Jobs told his audience exactly what it meant to them. For example, the audience learned that the video iPod is the best music player Apple has made, 30 percent thinner, 50 percent more storage capacity, has a "gorgeous" screen, and plays video as a bonus. Bottom line, said Jobs, the video iPod "will blow your mind." Jobs's style is to use over-the-top superlatives in his presentations, but they work because the audience—his customers—are at the center of the experience.

You don't need to be a CEO to sell the benefit to your listener. The technique applies to business professionals in any industry:

technology, manufacturing, services, real estate, even construction. I was once asked to speak to a group of custom homebuilders in Birmingham, Alabama. *Southern Living* magazine had arranged a conference for master craftsmen from around the country. When conference organizers asked me to keynote at their conference, I asked what I thought was a logical question: "I'm happy to speak to your group, but why would homebuilders be interested in a communications coach?" I learned that custom homebuilders are pitching themselves constantly to prospective customers, bankers, and real estate professionals. Skillfully motivating those listeners to back their projects could make the difference between a successful contractor and a struggling builder.

During a reception the night before the conference, I got the typical response when I asked people about themselves: "I'm a homebuilder in ... [fill in the city]." But one builder caught my attention. I asked what made him different from the other builders at the conference. Expecting to hear something about the quality of materials he uses, I was surprised when he told me, "In America, families need more togetherness time."

What does this have to do with constructing a home? I thought.

"I build homes with families in mind," he continued. "You'll find that my living areas are conducive to quality time. I bring families closer."

Then he launched into a discussion of his unique home designs. In less than thirty seconds, he had my full attention by focusing on the benefits—the advantages—of his style. He never mentioned wallboard, tiles, or fixtures. You see, for luxury homebuilders, using quality material is a given. But for this man, inspiring his customers required something more. It was a simple conversation that reinforced a profound technique.

My homebuilder friend was not pitching construction materials. He was pitching the idea of family togetherness. To inspire your listeners, constantly ask yourself, "What am I selling?" Think about it this way: Apple does not sell computers. It sells tools to unleash human potential. Starbucks does not sell coffee. It sells an experience, a "third place" between work and home. Cisco does not sell networking equipment. It sells human connections that change the way we live, work, play, and learn. And you might be surprised to know that Clorox does not sell bleach. It sells a clean, healthier home. What are you selling? I bet it is not the obvious.

There is a saying in the insurance industry that every year, 6 million quarter-inch drills are sold, and yet nobody wants a quarter-inch drill; they want a quarter-inch hole. In other words, people are looking for solutions to their problems. They are buying benefits, not products. Features like duration of coverage, level premiums, and cash value do not persuade customers to buy term life insurance. Life insurance customers are buying a family's gratitude. They are buying an education for their children should they pass away unexpectedly. They are buying little red wagons, toys, clothes, books, and birthday party favors. They are buying a spouse's peace of mind that the family's needs will be met. In *You, Inc.*, Harry Beckwith writes, "A great presentation must be motivational. . . . Great presentations are not intellectual; they are spiritual. You must reach the heart and soul. Effective financial planners do not sell you on quadrupling your money in twenty-five years; they sell the feeling you will experience when you do."[12]

What "feeling" do you want your customers or clients to experience after you pitch them a new product or service? What "feeling" do you want your employees to take away from your staff meeting? What "feeling" do you want to leave a recruiter with after an interview for your dream job? Enthusiasm and vision are important, but all the passion and mission in the world will not make up for a lack of empathy. When you speak, identify with your customers' pain and offer up a solution. Improve *their* lives and watch yourself succeed.

CHAPTER 4

Paint a Picture

Tell Powerful, Memorable, and Actionable Stories

A key—perhaps the key—to garnering a following is the effective communication of a story.

—Howard Gardner

"Twenty-two years ago my husband, Drew, and I began growing organic raspberries in our 2 1/2-acre garden and selling them from a roadside stand."[1] This is how Myra Goodman launches into the story of how she and her husband started living their lifelong dream to grow organic food. During the past two decades, the company they founded, Earthbound Farm, has become the largest grower of organic produce in North America. I met Myra as she prepared for a round of television interviews to promote her cookbook, *Food to Live By*. Her commitment to the organic lifestyle and her dedication to preserving the environment are unassailable. She is also quite persuasive.

Myra inspires her listeners by telling personal stories to either reinforce her commitment to the organic lifestyle or drive home a key message about the nutritional and environmental benefits of produce grown free of synthetic fertilizers and chemicals. Some time ago, Myra and Drew had grown "tired" of telling the same story over and over, especially the account of how they started selling raspberries at a roadside stand in Carmel, California. Internal research convinced them to stick to the story of their roots. In fact, focus group participants who were told the story of how Earthbound got started were much more receptive to the company's message than those who did not hear the story. Test groups had a positive reaction to the story of humble beginnings and hardworking values. It demonstrates the couple's passion, dedication, and staying power. (They opened their roadside stand in 1984.) Respondents said the story left them with a "sense of warmth" and "good feelings." Myra and Drew may have been sick of telling the same story, but it connected with their customers.

Inspiring individuals sell themselves, their vision, and their values by turning their message into a story that piques your interest, keeps you entertained, makes it easy to remember key points, and, above all, leads you to take some sort of action. Your message is not a story. You might have three points to get across during a new client meeting; those are your key messages. How you *structure* those messages represents your story. Do not confuse personal anecdotes with stories either. Anecdotes are rhetorical devices that should be included as elements in effective storytelling. Your "story" is much broader: A presentation tells a story, as does a sales pitch, a staff meeting, or a short conversation at a trade show booth. Stories take place everyday in the business world. Some are short, some are long, and some are too long! The goal of every story, however, is the same: to captivate your listeners.

The most astonishing speakers have mastered Simple Secret #4: They are skilled in telling powerful, memorable, and actionable stories. Since so few business professionals appreciate this skill, mastering the art of painting verbal pictures will set you apart from your competition. Some of my clients spend countless hours and tens of thousands of dollars on producing the show around a presentation: the conference room location and the production elements like sound and lighting. But research tells us that listeners recall very little of what is said in most presentations precisely because so little effort is spent on creating a captivating storyline. Tell better stories and your audience will be more inclined to take the action you desire.

Some people think telling a better story involves spending more time creating a "cool" PowerPoint show. That's not it. When Microsoft created the "animation scheme" tab in PowerPoint, the company didn't realize just how harmful it would become. The same can be said for Whitney Houston's decision to marry Bobby Brown—not a smart move. To Houston, it might have seemed like a good idea at the time, but she was committing career suicide. Avoid dying in your next presentation by animating the story and not the slides. Presentation software is a powerful tool when used correctly, but your story must get top billing.

A Convenient Lesson in Storytelling

Al Gore is the man who "used to be the next President of the United States," as he likes to joke. But his latest mission is all serious. Since 1989, Gore has given an estimated 1,000 presentations on global warming. Greenhouse gases—full of carbon dioxide—are being pumped into the atmosphere at alarming rates, he argues, and have already resulted in major climate changes. Gore warns that we could be heading for disaster if individuals, companies, and politicians fail to act. Producer Laurie David attended one of Gore's lectures and was so blown away by the presentation, she decided to turn it into a documentary: *An Inconvenient Truth*. The documentary won an Academy Award in 2007. While there was some editing involved to make the movie look like a documentary, at its core, *An Inconvenient Truth* is simply a presentation; one that is compelling and offers a valuable lesson in how to paint a picture through persuasive storytelling techniques. The presentation succeeds because it adheres to the elements of a great story, and great stories are what great films are made of.

The Greek System

The ancient Greeks were the first to discover the power of language to persuade and to study it as a science. The word "rhetoric" (persuasion through language) is derived from the Greek word for orator or teacher. You may be familiar with Aristotle and Plato, but a bunch of other guys with cool names also played a role in the development of persuasive language: Empedocles, Corax, Gorgias, and Isocrates. According to "Presentations and the Ancient Greeks," an article in the *Harvard Management Communication Letter*, "The Greek outline for a persuasive speech . . . has never been significantly improved upon. It is the chief insight the Greeks have to offer that can still significantly strengthen your presentation today, 2,500 years later."[2] The Greek rhetorical structure was made up of five parts: introduction, narrative, argument, refutation, and conclusion. Each of these elements can be applied to Gore's presentation.[3]

INTRODUCTION

You may have heard this common advice on giving a presentation: Begin by telling people what you are going to tell them, tell them, and then tell them what you just told them. It's time to reconsider this advice. "The Greeks believed, as countless audiences have since found, that such an approach is boring," according to the Harvard authors.[4] A better technique is to grab the attention of your audience by making an emotional connection with them through personal stories and observations.

In *An Inconvenient Truth*, Gore begins his presentation by setting the stage for his argument. In a series of colorful photographs of the earth taken from various space missions, he not only gets audiences to appreciate the beauty of our planet, but displays images that show how landmasses fit together at one time. Gore reminds his listeners that popular wisdom once held that the continents were never connected. Quoting Mark Twain, Gore says, "What gets us into trouble is not what we don't know, it's what we know for sure that just ain't so." The introduction is intended to remind listeners that assumptions they make today about global warming may not be accurate. The striking images make an emotional connection between Gore and his audience. Everyone starts on the same page—with an appreciation for the beauty of the planet. This approach allows listeners to be receptive to Gore's message as he leads into part two of the Greek structure.

Just as a great novelist would not divulge the plot outline in the first page, Gore doesn't reveal everything in the first two minutes. He lets the story evolve.

THE NARRATIVE

"Here you must get to the heart of the matter, whether it involves something you want your listeners to do, something you wish to per-suade them of, or something you want to tell them about," according to "Presentations and the Ancient Greeks."[5] The narrative lends itself to the telling of stories that reflect the essence of your presentation. Gore shares several anecdotes during his lecture, the most powerful and memorable of which involves the role tobacco played in his family and how it changed his way of thinking:

> When I was a kid, summertime meant working with tobacco. Working with the guys on the farm seemed like fun to me. Starting in 1964 with the Surgeon General's report, the evidence was laid out on the connection between smoking cigarettes and lung cancer. But we kept growing tobacco. My sister Nancy was ten years older than me and there were only the two of us. She was my protector and friend at the same time. She started smoking when she was a teenager and never stopped. She died of lung cancer. That's one of the ways you don't

want to die. The idea that we had been part of that economic pattern that produced the cigarettes that produced the cancer was so painful on so many levels. My father had grown tobacco all his life. Whatever explanation that seemed to make sense in the past just didn't cut it anymore. He stopped. It's human nature to take time to connect the dots. I know that. But I also know there can be a day of reckoning when you wish you had connected the dots more quickly.

The story is highly personal and memorable. It also serves an important purpose. Much like Gore's introduction, it reinforces the heart of his message, to challenge assumptions. Once he makes a connection with his listener through the telling of a personal story, Gore is ready for part three of the Greek structure.

THE ARGUMENT

This is the part of any presentation that could be really boring or exceptionally dazzling. In the argument, you present the proofs for your thesis, or message. Since scientific proof is required to persuade listeners of his point of view, Gore's presentation is supported by graphs, charts, statistics, and facts. But while most climate scientists would probably put the average listener to sleep with mind-numbing jargon and proof points, Gore carefully balances the need to inform and to entertain. Yes, entertain. Some elements of Gore's presentations are clearly intended to lighten up what could be a dry, scientific subject. The result is an even closer engagement between the speaker and his audience.

In one slide, Gore shows two overlapping line graphs; one represents carbon dioxide (CO_2) emissions in the atmosphere over the last 650,000 years while the second represents the average temperature of the earth in the same period. Both synchronize perfectly. In the next slide, Gore shows the line chart representing CO_2 climbing to the highest level in our planet's history, which represents where the level is today. "Now if you'll bear with me, I want to really emphasize this next point," Gore says as he climbs onto a mechanical lift. He presses a button and the lift carries him up at least five feet. He is now parallel with the point on the graph representing current CO_2 emissions. His actions elicit a small laugh from his audience. This bit is funny and insightful at the same time. "In less than fifty years," he goes on to say, "it's going to continue to go up. When some of these children who are here are my age, here's where it's going to be . . ." At this point, Gore presses the button again and the lift carries him higher for about ten seconds. As he is tracking the graph upward, he turns to the audience and says, "You've heard of off the charts? Well, here's where we're going to be in less than fifty years."

Most people remember this scene in the documentary. They may not recall the exact statistics Gore talks about it, but they remember his point. The more memorable a story, the more powerful and actionable it becomes. Gore takes data and brings it to life. The stage is now set for Gore to enter the fourth part of the Greek structure.

THE REFUTATION

In this part of the presentation, it is important to bring up the objections or counterarguments and shoot them down, especially if the topic is controversial. Gore says that one misconception perpetrated by skeptics is that scientists do not agree that the problem is real. He tackles criticism by citing one study of 928 peer-reviewed articles conducted on global warming over the last ten years. "Do you know the number of those [articles] that disagreed with the scientific consensus that we are causing global warming and that it's a serious problem? Out of the 928? Zero," says Gore. "The misconception that there is disagreement about this science has been deliberately created by a relatively small group of people." Throughout the presentation, Gore mixes facts, history, and humor to take a John Daley-size swing at his critics. It also sets up his audience for the fifth and final stage of the Greek structure.

THE FINALE

This is where a leader makes an appeal, a call to action. This appeal must be powerful, planned, memorized, and memorable. "Each one of us is a cause of global warming, but each one of us can make choices to change that with the things we buy, the electricity we use, the cars we drive; we can make choices to bring our individual carbon emissions to zero. The solutions are in our hands, we just have to have the determination to make it happen," says Gore. At this point, Gore delivers a memorable quote, a quote he repeats consistently in presentations and in his acceptance speech at the Academy Awards: "We have everything that we need to reduce carbon emissions, everything but political will. But in America, the will to act is a renewable resource." This is the last line in his presentation, and one of the most memorable.

Whether you are liberal or conservative, Democrat or Republican, a believer or a skeptic, few can disagree that Gore presents a strong case. The *Los Angeles Times* called the movie a "highly persuasive documentary."[6] There is a considerable amount of debate over just how damaging global warming will be for our planet, but my goal is not to debate the issue; nor should you read any political bias where there is none. Gore is a master storyteller who has something to teach us about creating persuasive presentations. Regardless of our political affiliations, we should listen.

The Road from Flip Charts to the Academy Awards

As I worked on this manuscript, I had the opportunity to meet the designers at the firm that created Gore's presentation. Prior to tapping Duarte Design in Mountain View, California, Gore used 35mm slides and flip charts to present his material.[7] Duarte took

Gore's information and turned it into a captivating multimedia presentation.

Duarte's brilliant team of designers has a unique approach to creating presentations that inspire and motivate. Here is the company's advice for turning presentations into visual stories:

1. *Create one point per slide.* Stick to one idea on one slide. Resist the temptation to tell the audience everything you know at once.
2. *Treat the audience as king.* The audience doesn't want to hear about you. They want to know what's in it for them. Give them a reason for taking their time and make sure there's a payoff at the end. This is one of the reasons why I recommend losing the "About Us" slide at the beginning of most presentations. It's not about you; it's about them.
3. *Make the invisible visible.* Don't just present mountains of raw data. Create compelling visuals that will help the audience reach an "epiphany" moment—an insight or "aha" that hits the audience dead on. Earlier I mentioned the key slide in Gore's presentation, which arrives about twenty minutes into the movie: a simple red line graph that goes up and down shows carbon dioxide emissions in the atmosphere over 650,000 years. A second line appears (in blue) that shows the average temperature of the earth over the same period. The two lines correlate. Gore summarizes the slide simply by saying: "When there is more carbon dioxide, the temperature gets warmer." Where most presenters would have put the data into tables with a bevy of complicated numbers, Gore helps the audience reach an epiphany by making the invisible visible. Before creating the slides, the designers had asked themselves, "What is the data trying to tell us?" It wasn't the data points that the audience needed to see, but the correlation the data prove.

(*continued*)

4. *Have a Spielberg moment.* Consider a presentation as a way to evoke an emotional response. Duarte presentations have ebbs and flows. They build up to key moments, offering surprises and twists, like great movies. The presentations keep people emotionally drawn to the speaker and the story. Animators call this storytelling "time-based content": Information is revealed over time instead of dumping a ton of information on the listener at once.

5. *Maintain a visual-verbal balance.* Duarte designers make sure presentations have the right mix of visuals to compliment and not compete with the speaker. At some points during a presentation, the audience's attention should be focused on the slide while at other points, the speaker and what she has to say takes center stage.

6. *Practice design, not decorating.* Design is intended to make your message clear, not to generate false excitement about your data. Do not "exhaust the eyeballs" with needless animation, according to designers.

The $253 Million Story

On August 22, 2005, drug giant Merck was ordered to pay $253 million in punitive damages to Carol Ernst, whose husband, Robert, had died four years earlier after taking the arthritis painkiller Vioxx. By a vote of ten to two, a Texas jury found Merck to be negligent, and awarded $24 million for Carol's mental anguish and $229 million in punitive damages. The size of the punitive damage shocked many observers. Merck's attorneys maintained that the company acted responsibly and that there was no reliable scientific evidence that Vioxx had anything to do with the man's death. It was the first case involving the painkiller. As of this writing, Merck is appealing the verdict and has won some other product liability cases on this issue. But the victory in the Texas case is a testament to the power of persuasive speaking.

Houston trial lawyer Mark Lanier argued the case. As the son of a minister (and a part-time minister himself), Lanier appreciates the power of a good story. Lanier made the case that Merck knew about the health risks associated with Vioxx but concealed the information to protect its profits. Merck insisted that Vioxx did not cause Robert's death, and blamed it on an arrhythmia—an irregular heartbeat—instead of a heart attack brought on by the medication.

Lanier persuaded the jury by the power of his storytelling—a story aided by a groundbreaking PowerPoint show to supplement his opening argument. The slide show was so convincing that some reporters covering the trial called it "frighteningly powerful." PowerPoint expert Cliff Atkinson helped Lanier develop the story. I spent some time with Atkinson to get a better understanding of how the team succeeded in telling a persuasive story. According to Atkinson:

> When a reporter interviewed jurors after the verdict, one member of the jury said when the defense talked about the science behind its drug, it went over their heads. It was unintelligible, sort of like the character in the Peanuts cartoon who, when she talks, all that comes out of her mouth is "wha wha wha." In contrast, Mark's explanation was clear and understandable. When we conducted a follow-up six months later, we discovered that the jurors had remembered Mark's opening statement and the images he used. The story was burned into their minds. They could repeat the story back to us![8]

A PRESENTATION TO REMEMBER

Atkinson believes in creating an emotional connection with the listener in the first few slides, or "frames," of a presentation. He does this by setting up the story, establishing a protagonist (the lead character), defining the problem, and showing the solution. Together Lanier and Atkinson used this structure to create the opening argument, transforming 3 million court documents, hours of depositions, and thousands of pages of scientific data into a simple, easy-to-follow story that eventually led jurors down one path and to one conclusion: Merck concealed information about the potentially harmful effects of the drug to protect its profits. With Atkinson's and Lanier's permission, I have included the first six slides of the presentation, along with Atkinson's explanation of how each slide added a new dimension to the story.

Frame 1. The first slide shows a happy couple, Carol and Robert Ernst. Carol was a single mother raising four children when she met Robert. Carol's daughter had introduced them. They fell in love and were married. Carol and Robert were happily married for one year before something happened that would change everything. This slide establishes the setting. (See Figure 4.1.)

Figure 4.1   Carol and Robert Ernst are happy to have found each other. PowerPoint Slide for Merck trial, 2005. Courtesy of Cliff Atkinson and W. Mark Lanier.

Figure 4.2 Something tragic happens to Carol and Robert Ernst. PowerPoint Slide for Merck trial, 2005. Courtesy of Cliff Atkinson and W. Mark Lanier.

Frame 2. The background disappears and turns white. Lanier tells the jurors that Bob died suddenly of a heart attack, leaving a hole in Carol's life. (See Figure 4.2.)

Frame 3. A chalk outline replaces the image of Bob. Here Lanier is reframing the story for a conservative Texas jury that might be reluctant to award large damages in a product liability case. Through prior questioning, Lanier learned that the jurors' favorite show was *CSI*. He uses that information to reframe the events into a murder case and will ask jurors to play detective. The jurors become the protagonists of the story, getting to sort through the evidence and ultimately to bring justice to Carol's family. (See Figure 4.3.)

Figure 4.3   Carol loses Robert.
PowerPoint Slide for Merck trial, 2005. Courtesy of Cliff Atkinson and W.
Mark Lanier.

Frame 4. This slide is the first of a three-part puzzle that Lanier will assemble for the jurors. All great stories have a protagonist, a hero, and an antagonist (an enemy to fight). Now that the jurors are empowered as the heroes, Merck is introduced as the enemy. Lanier tells them that his case will prove that a pharmaceutical giant called Merck produced a drug that it knew might increase the risk of heart attacks. Merck did not tell Bob's doctor. He took the drug and died of a heart attack. Lanier argues that Merck had reason to hide the information from the public: millions of dollars. The company had a "motive." (See Figure 4.4.)

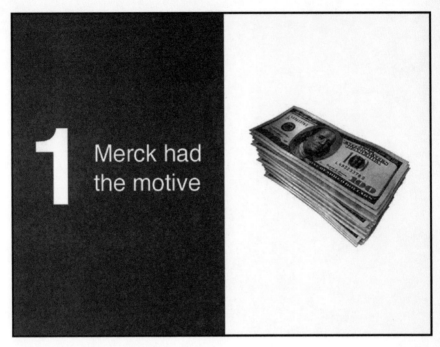

Figure 4.4 Merck's motive.
PowerPoint Slide for Merck trial, 2005. Courtesy of Cliff Atkinson and W. Mark Lanier.

Frame 5. A simple photo of two Vioxx pills. Lanier argues that the pills were the weapon, the "means" to commit the crime the jurors were empowered to solve. (See Figure 4.5.)

Frame 6. This last slide shows Carol alongside Bob's outline with the words "Motive and means cause death." Lanier has pieced together a simple puzzle for the jurors. All of the facts, science, testimony, and evidence they will hear in the weeks ahead can now be placed in the context of the story that Lanier has framed. (See Figure 4.6.)

Atkinson looks at a story from the perspective of a blockbuster movie. "Hollywood has been communicating with words and pictures

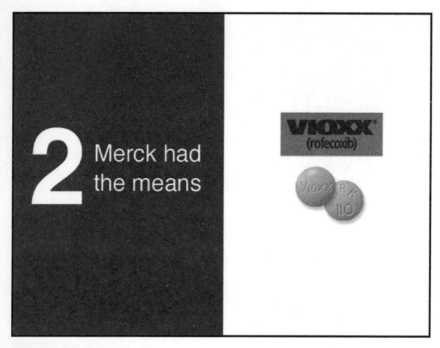

Figure 4.5 Vioxx pills.
PowerPoint Slide for Merck trial, 2005. Courtesy of Cliff Atkinson and W. Mark Lanier.

for one hundred years," says Atkinson.[9] Hollywood tells stories, but most PowerPoint presentations do not. Atkinson argues that the way most people have been using PowerPoint for the last twenty years does not work. He makes a persuasive case for completely reinventing the way presenters use the tool to tell a story. In Atkinson's book, *Beyond Bullet Points*, he writes, "If you're like most people who use PowerPoint, creating a presentation starting with a series of bullet points is probably second nature . . . but although bullet points make it easy for us to create slides, they don't always make it easy for audiences to understand what we want to say."[10]

Atkinson told me that the legal industry was the first to really take advantage of his three-step storytelling structure. "There's no doubt

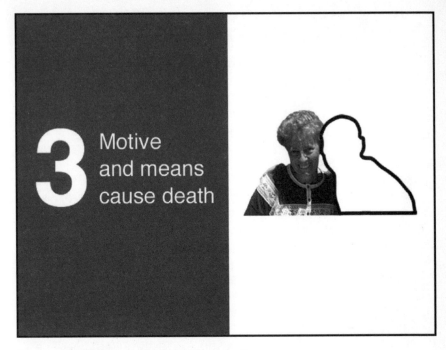

Figure 4.6 Motive and means cause death.
PowerPoint Slide for Merck trial, 2005. Courtesy of Cliff Atkinson and W. Mark Lanier.

among lawyers about the need to tell a story, but among businesspeople, not everyone is there yet. They all don't see the need to make information understandable in the form of a story."[11] Persuading individuals to follow a desired course of action requires an emotional engagement with the listener. The Merck defense team overwhelmed jurors with mind-numbing statistics, studies, and jargon; the winning team framed the case as a simple narrative so convincing that the outcome was perfectly clear.

Most clients who contact me to improve their speaking and communication style have already created a presentation and want to deliver it with more charisma. As Lanier and Atkinson have proven, a charismatic speaking style begins well before a presentation has been

Three Steps to Telling a Story with PowerPoint

Cliff Atkinson says no Hollywood movie director would begin filming without a script. Great movies begin as storyboards, and Atkinson believes great presentations should follow suit.

Step 1. Write your story before you even open PowerPoint. Spend most of your time and energy here. Atkinson recommends that speakers put their audience in the center of the story by introducing a problem they face and how you will solve it. Recall in Chapter 3 when I suggested eliminating the "About Us" slide from the start of most presentations: Setting the stage for the listener means focusing on the problem faced by your audience. In Step 1, speakers are encouraged to create the three or four top-level messages they want to get across during their presentations, along with supporting points and subpoints. Speakers should write out these points as complete sentences.

Step 2. Here each key message becomes a headline for a PowerPoint slide. Just as each scene gets its own storyboard before shooting begins in a Hollywood movie, each message gets its own slide or scene. Then you should illustrate each headline with a simple graphic, *not* with bullet points.

Step 3. Atkinson calls this stage "producing the experience." PowerPoint is just one tool in the presentation arsenal. What other tools will you be using? Flip charts, whiteboards, handouts, demonstrations? All of these elements create an engaging "experience." Rehearsal is also a key part of this stage. The PowerPoint slides should advance seamlessly as you give voice to your story. Rehearsal involves interacting smoothly with the slides and your audience. If each slide has only a headline and a graphic, the audience has no choice but to focus on the speaker. How you talk, move, and make contact with the audience becomes more important than ever.

Atkinson's approach represents a complete makeover, an overhaul of the way most of us use PowerPoint. His book, *Beyond Bullet Points*, presents a detailed step-by-step guide to his storyboarding technique.

created. It begins with the narrative. Write your story before producing it!

Wowing 'Em at the Ritz

Every day at each of more than 65 Ritz-Carlton hotels in twenty-one countries, in each department, on every shift, employees are called in for a "lineup." According to the Ritz-Carlton president, Simon Cooper (whom we will hear more from in Chapter 5), the lineup is one of the most important tools the hotel brand offers to its employees to reinforce the values and actions it expects everyone to demonstrate.[12] The lineup is a fifteen-minute pep talk where everyone shares "wow" stories. Wow stories feature hotel employees who create unique, memorable, and personal experiences for guests. A housekeeper who shows up for the evening shift in Shanghai will hear the same story as a doorman had heard in Hong Kong an hour earlier or a waiter in New York the next morning. Here is one example of a real "wow" story read and circulated among the staff. It is reprinted here with the Ritz-Carlton's permission.

Today's wow story is from The Ritz-Carlton, San Juan Hotel, Spa & Casino and demonstrates today's Service Value 1 in building strong relationships to create Ritz-Carlton guests for life.[13]

A married couple had been repeat guests at the hotel for the past few years. This year, a suit the wife was wearing was stained due to a spill on the counter. It was a very expensive suit and it was sent immediately to the Laundry to be dry-cleaned. The stain, however, would not come out. The guest was very disappointed when she checked out, as nothing could be done to restore her ruined suit. Harold Rodriquez, Laundry Supervisor, called her home to apologize and asked if she was willing to FedEx her suit so that another attempt could be made to remove the stain from the suit. The guest agreed and

Harold contacted an external laundry company for their assistance. Harold called the guest every day to keep her informed on the progress of the suit cleaning. Unfortunately, the outside laundry company was unable to remove the stain.

Harold wanted to turn the situation around and build a relationship for life with the guests. He therefore proceeded to get the cost of the suit reimbursed, took the check, got on a plane to New York, drove to their home, and rang the doorbell. When he introduced himself, the couple looked surprised. Harold received smiles and hugs. Their gratitude was priceless. He had created a memorable experience for the guests by turning a problem into an opportunity to "wow" them with genuine care and service excellence. His belief that nothing is impossible: when you do something from the heart everything in life can be accomplished. First class to Harold for enlivening Service Value 1!

If you find this story hard to believe, rest assured it is true. The hotel employees—the "ladies and gentlemen" of the Ritz-Carlton—are inspired to provide an exceptional level of service to their guests based largely on the way leadership communicates its values and expectations in the form of stories. "It's the best way to communicate what we expect from our ladies and gentlemen around the world," says Cooper. "Every story reinforces the actions we are looking for and demonstrates how each and every person in our organization contributes to our service values."

Stories have the power to inspire, motivate, and persuade anyone in everyday situations. "Stories speak to both parts of the human mind—its reason and emotion," writes Howard Gardner.[14] Stories should not be reserved for the former vice president of the United States speaking on the topic of global warming or a famous attorney arguing one of the most nationally followed product liability trials in history. Stories speak to all of us and should be used in every situation in which the goal is to paint a picture for an individual, team, or company, a picture of a desired outcome.

Analogies, Metaphors, and Other Tools to Jazz Up Your Story

The ancient Greek structure outlined earlier has stood the test of time because it reaches people on a logical level; but within the structure, as Cliff Atkinson and Howard Gardner point out, there is plenty of room to strike an emotional chord with your listeners. We tend to forget much of what we hear, but we remember 100 percent of what we *feel*. Connect to people's hearts by using the techniques described next; they are effective in any form of communication, from a formal presentation to a casual conversation.

ANALOGIES

An analogy is a similarity between the like features of two things. Analogies help us understand concepts that might be foreign to us. For example, Intel spokespeople have decided that when they explain the inner workings of a microprocessor to general audiences, the most powerful analogy is "The computer chip is the brain of your computer." In many ways the chip serves the same function in the computer as a brain serves in a human. The chip and the brain are two different things with similar features. This one analogy is so useful, it is widely picked up by the media. When you find one strong analogy that works, stick to it!

SIMILES

The most persuasive leaders I have met tend to use similes frequently in their professional communications (i.e., interviews, meetings, presentations, or pitches). Similes are figures of speech comparing two unlike things using the words "like" or "as." They are cool and clear, and you can have a lot of fun with them.

During a commencement address at the University of Pennsylvania, U2's Bono said, "I don't think there's anything more unseemly than the sight of a rock star in academic robes. It's a bit like when people put their King Charles spaniels in little tartan sweats and hats. It's not natural, and it doesn't make the dog any smarter."[15] That's a simile! It makes an experience more vivid. If you help me as the listener visualize a concept, I am more likely to see it in my mind's eye and to feel it. Remember, it is easier for listeners to act on something they feel, something they recall vividly.

Al Gore uses plenty of similes in his global warming presentation. When describing what melting ice looks like in Antarctica, Gore says, "What happens is the water tunnels to the bottom and makes the ice like Swiss cheese, sort of like termites." Actually that's two in one sentence! I've never been to Antarctica and probably never will until they build a Hyatt there, but I know what Swiss cheese looks like. In this case, the simile makes Gore's message more vivid.

METAPHORS

Metaphors are close cousins to similes but a bit trickier. Metaphors are a comparison between two things that are seemingly unrelated; they describe one thing as another. When former New York governor Mario Cuomo called America a "shining city on a hill," for example, he was creating a metaphor. During my research into the Ritz-Carlton, I read that one manager described working at the hotel as "playing on the varsity team." He would tell his new employees, "This isn't a scrimmage or a junior varsity game. You are in the big time now, performing at a level far beyond your previous experience." The manager was using a metaphor to emotionally engage employees by relating their new experience to something with which they may be more familiar.

Metaphors are the core of memory, according to Gerald Zaltman in *How Customers Think*. "[Metaphors] help us see new connections, interpret our experiences, and draw new meaning from those experiences. Metaphors also affect imagination. . . . speaking metaphorically, metaphor is the engine of imagination."[16] This is a powerful endorsement for the use of metaphors in your communications. Zaltman argues that emotion is a stronger influence in a buying decision than logical reasoning, and that is why metaphors are so important: When you use metaphors and visual imagery to help describe your product, you make your product memorable and stimulate your listeners' imagination, creating that emotional connection required for persuasion. Language scholars have discovered that charismatic communicators like Ronald Reagan use more metaphors in their speeches than less inspiring communicators. If metaphors work for the Great Communicator, they will work for us!

STEP INSIDE MY METAPHOR

I once visited a company where the entire office space represented a metaphor for the founders' philosophy. You might recall my conversation with Mike McCue, the visionary CEO of Tellme Networks, whom I interviewed for Chapter 3. When I first drove up to the building, I thought Google Maps had given me the wrong directions, which would have been a first and a big disappointment. There was no obvious sign on the side of the building. I was looking for a grand entrance and a marble-tiled lobby that would reflect the big bucks the company was generating. I found no such thing. Instead, a small sign pointed to the back of the building and a door next to "Shipping and Delivery." My first thought was that the company must not have been as successful as I had assumed. As I walked through a rather plain lobby, the doors opened to a cavernous space with no offices and no cubicles. The desks were arranged in pods where individuals work together in groups. This setup, I was informed, fosters learning. Engineers can ask questions of marketers, marketers can ask questions of engineers, and everyone can ask questions of the CEO, who occupies a space in one of the pods. The funniest thing about the desks is that they are not "desks" at all. The workspaces are crafted out of wooden doors, straight from a home improvement store. You can even see the holes where the doorknobs should be!

There is a reason behind the madness. The entire space acts as a metaphor to remind everyone that the company started modestly, literally in a small office next to Shipping and Receiving. Nobody gets cubicles or offices because there is no "caste system" at Tellme. The company believes that no one should get a larger cubicle with cherry-wood trim because they have a higher position, so there are no cubicles. The office is a metaphor for a team, and everyone plays an integral part. The metaphor is so ingrained in the corporate culture that the receptionist who welcomed me could tell me all about the location of the office and the reason behind the unique workspace. Metaphors are powerful and memorable.

The Goldilocks Metaphor

When I worked as a business journalist for CNN in New York, reporters would always go back to the same handful of economists for quotes, or "sound bites." The best economists spoke in metaphors to make the subject easy to understand. For example, the financial press loves talking about the Goldilocks economy—one that's not too hot and not too cold. This is the best-case scenario, because if the economy is running too hot and growth is too strong, the Federal Reserve will raise interest rates to slow it down. When an economy grows too slowly, however, jobs are lost and the nation could plunge into the "icy bath" of recession.

TRIADS

I love triads. You will find many in my books, columns and presentations. Research shows we can easily remember items in groups of three. My own focus groups bear this out; listeners tend to remember three key points the speaker is trying to make, but not much more. Try to give them four, five, or six main points, and they forget everything. When the English were being attacked by the Nazis during World War II, imagine how inspired they must have felt when they heard Winston Churchill say, "We will fight them on the beaches, we will fight them on the streets and in our towns, and we will fight them in our homes." Churchill was a big fan of triads.

I once worked with the head of sales for a large, high-tech company. His goal was to get his sales team fired up about the new fiscal year. He began by outlining a very long agenda for the afternoon. I asked him to throw out the agenda, face the audience, and simply state the three most important messages they should take away from the day. He thought about it for a moment and decided on this for his opener: "Thank you for coming today. I'm really excited because there are a lot of new initiatives, ideas, products, and information you'll be hearing about today, but there are three things I hope you take away from it: Number one: This will be the best year in our company's history. Number two: We have signed the largest retail agreement ever for our company, and its implications are enormous. And finally, for most of you, this will be the most lucrative year of your career!" The sales staff was thrilled. They cheered, had smiles on their faces, and were eager to learn more. Fast forward one year later. Everything came true. It was the best year for the company, and the bonuses were historic. It was not the content of his original presentation that was boring, but the way he presented it. Remember the rule of three when speaking, presenting, and delivering your message.

ANAPHORA

This literary tool is another one of those rhetorical devices we have
to thank the ancient Greeks for. This one is very cool and has a lot
of impact. Anaphora is simply repeating the same words or phrase at
the beginning of several consecutive sentences. One of the more famous examples came from Martin Luther King Jr.'s "I Have a Dream"
speech: "I have a dream that one day this nation will rise up and live out
the true meaning of its creed. . . . I have a dream that my four little children will one day live in a nation where they will not be judged by the
color of their skin but by the content of their character. I have a dream
today." Even if you heard the entire speech, you would probably most
remember the "I have a dream" sequence. That's anaphora at its best!

Corporate leaders often use this technique to rally their employees.
You can just imagine a CEO saying "Our competitor says they make
a better product than us. We will prove them wrong! Our competitor
says they'll take market share away from us. We will prove them wrong!
Our competitor says customers will prefer their product. We will prove
them wrong!"

BALANCE

This final technique takes more thought and should be used only
sparingly, but when it is done well, it is absolutely mesmerizing. The
technical term is not "balance," but "chiasmus." It is a strange word, so
for the sake of simplicity, we will call it balance. You know it when you
hear it. When John F. Kennedy said, "Ask not what your country can do
for you, ask what you can do for your country," he gave us an example
of balance. Ted Sorensen, who wrote Kennedy's inaugural speech of
January 20, 1961, had a real thing for chiasmus. The speech contains
several examples, including this famous line: "Let us never negotiate
out of fear, but let us never fear to negotiate." Country singers seem

to like this technique, too. One of my favorite country artists, Brad Paisley, had a hit in 2006 with the hook: "To the world, you may be just another girl, but to me, baby you are the world!"[17]

Stories for the Soul

I was not surprised when Barbara Walters picked evangelist Joel Osteen as one of the ten most fascinating people in 2006. I watch Osteen's sermons on television and on the Internet and am captivated by his ability to inspire his audience through the use of many of the techniques you have learned so far. His stories have the power to electrify 40,000 people a week who visit Houston's Lakewood church to hear him speak as well as the 7 million weekly viewers who watch on television. His stories are short; sometimes they are personal, other times they are not. But Osteen's stories always reinforce his theme and help his listeners recall the message of the day long after they have left the building.

I recall one sermon in which Osteen urged his listeners to stretch to the next level, saying that too many people are living below their potential. Osteen said:

> I was reading about Frank Lloyd Wright. He was a famous architect. Designed many beautiful buildings, many magnificent structures. Toward the end of his career, a reporter asked him, of all the many beautiful designs, which one was his favorite? Without missing a beat, he said, "My next one." ... You may have had some dreams come to pass, but we have to enlarge our vision for the new things on the horizon. That means if you're a teacher, you haven't taught your best lesson yet. If you're a builder, you haven't built your best home yet. If you're a business person, you haven't cut your best deal yet.[18]

By telling a simple story about Frank Lloyd Wright (using a triad and anaphora in the process), Osteen helps his listeners paint a picture, imagining themselves climbing new mountains and pursuing new dreams. Osteen tells stories in every sermon because stories bring the message to life. Stories have the power to lift us up, give us hope, and paint a vivid picture of what we are trying to accomplish for our teams, organizations, families, or ourselves. Anyone can deliver a message, but inspiring speakers tell stories. Tell more of them and you will set yourself on the path to inspiring others.

CHAPTER 5

Invite Participation

Solicit Input, Overcome Objections, and Develop a Winning Strategy

Most of the successful people I've known are the ones who do more listening than talking.

—Bernard Baruch

I once asked a newspaper reporter, whose job allowed him to meet famous personalities around the world, whom he had enjoyed meeting the most, the one person who inspired him above all others. "Bill Clinton," he said without hesitation. The reporter had had the opportunity to meet President Clinton after hearing him speak in South Africa. The two spent only three minutes together, but Clinton left an impression that will last a lifetime. "His gaze never left my eyes," the reporter told me. "He made me feel as though I was the most important person in the room at that moment; even more important than Bill Gates, who was standing right next to us!"

The key to selling yourself, your vision, and your values is not to "announce" them but to get others to embrace them. But it is not enough to keep your mouth shut and your ears open. Yes, people want to know that you are listening to them, but Simple Secret #5

Figure 5.1 Cartoon by Scott Adams. Courtesy of Dilbert © Scott Adams, distributed by United Feature Syndicate, Inc.

calls for opening a dialogue with people; this means that you should include others and make them feel as if they are equal participants in projects that impact their lives. Listening is not enough. Asking for feedback, and taking action based on what you hear, makes all the difference. (See Figure 5.1.)

The Place Where You're Heard Is the Best Place to Work

Griffin Hospital in Derby, Connecticut, has consistently ranked as one of *Fortune* magazine's "100 Best Companies to Work."[1] Hospital leaders tell me that their secret to landing on this list for seven straight years is their policy of open and honest communication with staff and patients. It's that approach that inspires Griffin staff to perform their best and to revolutionize patient care in America. Griffin leadership solicits input from patients and staff alike and turns that information into tangible improvement initiatives that benefit everyone. Employees have a say in the way they treat others as well as the way they themselves are treated. The hospital's commitment to open and honest communication is what transformed Griffin from a hospital with big problems to a hospital solving big problems.

SURVIVING THE PERFECT STORM

In the early 1980s, Griffin's buildings were old, market share was declining, and good doctors were leaving. When nearby residents were asked "What hospital would you avoid?" one in three answered "Griffin." Add lower Medicare reimbursements to the mix and Griffin was facing a "perfect storm" that threatened its very existence. Griffin's transformation began in 1985 when the chief executive officer, Patrick Charmel, and the vice president, Bill Powanda decided that it was time to solicit input, overcome objections, and develop a winning strategy.

Beginning in January, the hospital held monthly retreats for 100 employees per session. During the retreats, participants were asked: "If you were a patient, or the family member of a patient, admitted to Griffin Hospital, what would you want the hospital experience to be like?" The answer was consistent in every group every month: They wanted a patient-centered experience that was the exact opposite of what the hospital had been delivering up to that point. That realization, or "aha," gave life to a new culture that would radically transform the hospital's approach to care and eventually make it a model for 120 other hospitals that have since followed suit.

GIVE PREGNANT WOMEN WHAT THEY WANT—*EVERYTHING* THEY WANT!

By 1987, soliciting input from staff, listening to what they had to say, and taking action based on those opinions had become so successful that Charmel decided to apply the technique to Griffin's customers: its patients. In 1987 Charmel was overseeing Griffin's first major renovation project: a new childbirth center. Instead of soliciting input from staff this time, he listened to women who had delivered at Griffin, pregnant women who had yet to decide where they would give birth, and those women who had chosen to give birth elsewhere. As the father of two girls, I know that asking a pregnant woman what she wants from a hospital is like asking a three-year-old what he wants for Christmas: You are bound to get a very long list! The wish list included: separate entrances (pregnant women do not consider themselves "sick"), female obstetricians, private rooms with bathrooms and showers, family rooms, double beds, and Jacuzzis.

Leaders and administrators at Griffin began meeting to review the list and set priorities, but Charmel startled the group by saying "If the original list identified everything that women wanted in the childbirth experience, then let's give it *all* to them!" Griffin did exactly that. The number of births at the hospital doubled during the next four years, exceeding 1,000 a year. More impressive was the fact that one of three women came from outside the community primarily served by the hospital. Patient satisfaction had soared to 100 percent. Griffin's new mantra became "Give the customer what they want; they shall come, and be very happy!"

OPEN AND HONEST COMMUNICATIONS GETS PUT TO THE TEST

According to Powanda, Griffin's policy of open and honest communications was to put to the test in November 2001.[2] It began on Friday, November 16, when an elderly woman was admitted to the hospital with mild dehydration and symptoms of an upper respiratory infection. Ninety-four-year-old Ottilie Lundgren's condition deteriorated rapidly, and she died several days later, becoming the nation's fifth victim of anthrax inhalation. The hospital lab had taken samples when Lundgren entered the hospital, and on Saturday morning an infectious disease physician noticed something strange in the culture. "It's inhalation anthrax," she told senior hospital leaders.

By Monday morning, all of the hospital's tests had returned positive for anthrax, but state and federal governments had to conduct their own tests. On Tuesday morning, Powanda and Charmel received a phone call from a shaken state inspector confirming the hospital's results. Charmel and Powanda had called a meeting for 3:30 that afternoon to inform the 400 day-shift employees of the situation, but the FBI had other plans: It wanted its agents to conduct their own tests before any announcement was made. The FBI spokesperson was adamant: The hospital was a crime scene, and the FBI would reconsider an announcement only after its own tests on Wednesday, a full six days after Lundgren had been admitted.

Shortly after hanging up with the FBI, Powanda received a call from Governor John Rowland, who also requested that the hospital cancel the staff meeting. Charmel and Powanda were beginning to wonder if the meeting was the right decision. They called a representative from the American Hospital Association, who said that if their situation had been taking place in any other hospital, he would have also recommended that the meeting be delayed. But Griffin was different: "If you do not follow the open and honest culture you have created at Griffin, you will destroy in one day what has taken you ten years to build." On Tuesday, November 20, Charmel held a staff meeting at the end of the day shift to communicate the facts behind the case, the tests, and how anthrax is spread.

Griffin went on to win an award from a local newspaper for its boldness and commitment to the public's right to know. Charmel's actions were nothing "short of heroic," according to New London Day.[3] A front-page story told the rest of the world what his colleagues already knew: Charmel had become a hero to his staff long before the anthrax crisis because he committed himself to making them all feel as if they played key roles in the hospital's success, which they most certainly do.

CARING STARTS IN THE PARKING LOT

Griffin leaders like Charmel have set a precedent with staff and provide a model for behavior that all employees—managers, doctors, nurses, and administrators alike—strive to emulate. Every employee is considered a "caregiver"—even the security guards, parking lot valets, and chefs—and they all feel comfortable addressing Charmel directly with praise, concerns, or suggestions. If an employee believes the hospital is failing to put the patient first in any area of care, Charmel is the first to know; he makes himself as available as possible. His lines of communication include:

- *A long day's walk.* Charmel spends most of the working day in the hospital, but out of his office. He typically starts office work after 5:00 p.m. because he meets with people in their own departments all day; they do not come to him. This is the ultimate open-door policy. It is not unusual to see employees chatting with Charmel in the hallway. They are confident that their concerns, observations, and ideas will not only be heard but acted on.

- *First impressions count.* Charmel welcomes all new employees with a two-hour presentation every month. This orientation is mandatory for all new employees and volunteers, and Charmel does not miss it; if he must, the orientation is rescheduled.

- *Open the books.* Twice a year Charmel hosts a "State of the Hospital" meeting for all employees and volunteers, where everyone hears exactly the same information as the board of directors: strategic information, market share data, financial statistics, and plans for the future. Everything.

- *Get them news quickly.* Charmel contributes to a daily newsletter, *Griffin Today*, which is distributed to 700 hospital workstations accessible to both employees and patients, and supplemented by an electronic newsletter.

- *The old-fashioned touch.* Charmel sends letters directly to the homes of employees and volunteers, about hospital, community, or medical issues as they directly affect them.

■ *Don't forget the customers.* At Griffin, patients become partners in their treatment and care. Patients are handed a packet of information within twenty-four hours of admission that contains articles and information about their medical problem. Patients can use the state-of-the-art Health Resource Center to learn more about their condition and symptoms, and conferences are held with the primary care nurse, attending physicians, social work staff, and the patient's family. Everyone has a voice. Griffin has learned that constant communication reduces patient anxiety.[4]

In addition to being named one of *Fortune*'s "Best Places to Work," Griffin ranks among the highest on a trust measurement used to identify the companies that make the *Fortune* list. (See Figure 5.2.) Employees say that they are informed about important issues, expectations are clear, and they hear straight answers to their questions. By informing everyone that they have a voice in patient care, Griffin has transformed the hospital experience for patients and employees alike.

Griffin teaches us that the world's most admired companies offer superior service, but extraordinary service cannot occur without engaged employees who participate in its creation and are inspired because they have been heard.

Unmasking The Ritz-Carlton Mystique

The Ritz-Carlton is synonymous with unparalleled service. Visit any Ritz-Carlton luxury hotel in more than twenty countries and you will be greeted with friendly, enthusiastic, and highly polished "Ladies and Gentlemen serving Ladies and Gentlemen." For more than twenty years "The Ritz-Carlton Basics" guided every interaction between employee and guests. These twenty rules dictated everything from exactly

Figure 5.2   CEO Patrick Charmel makes Griffin Hospital the "Best Place to Work." Griffin president and CEO Patrick Charmel addresses employees at annual State of the Hospital meeting.
Photo by Lisa Seaburg. Courtesy of Griffin Communications Department.

what to say (Never say "hello." Use more formal greetings like "Good morning") to actions (Never let a guest carry his own luggage). But as the world changed so did the typical Ritz-Carlton hotel guest. It was time to rethink the service values by letting employees think for themselves. In stepped President and Chief Operating Officer, Simon Cooper, who faced a communications challenge: Motivating more than 35,000 employees to adopt significant changes to the corporate culture. As I learned during an interview with Cooper, his approach was simple but powerfully inspirational.

Changing the Bible

Twenty years ago, the luxury traveler rewarded consistency. A hotel in Boston had to look the same as the one across the pond in Barcelona.

There was no mistaking the face of a guest: Caucasian, male, dressed in a suit and alone on business. The times they are "a changing" as the song goes. Walk into a lobby of a Ritz-Carlton hotel today and you will find younger guests, international travelers, and families. Most guests have swapped their pinstripes for khakis. The guest had changed and service had to change with them. According to Cooper, the Ritz-Carlton had done such a thorough job of training its staff to communicate with guests, the interactions could border on the mechanical. That was no longer desirable for a more casual traveler. Cooper knew it. He had to make sure the rest of The Ritz-Carlton hotel team would buy into it as well.

Cooper and senior leaders began a listening tour. They solicited input from everyone in the organization: managers to housekeepers. They listened. They repeated what they were hearing. They acted on the feedback. Front line employees were basically asking for more flexibility in the way they were allowed to interact with guests. By listening to both customers and employees, Cooper was being asked to tinker with "the Bible," the twenty rules that made up The Ritz-Carlton experience. Not everyone was in agreement. Some objected and for seemingly good reasons. You see, there was no obvious need to change. Customer scores were outstanding as well as employee satisfaction, profit growth, and expansion plans. Cooper, however, had a long history of experience in the luxury hotel business. He knew that what he was hearing may have seemed unnecessary to many observers, but failing to act could jeopardize the brand long term.

We were world class by any metric you could use to judge us by. That is where leadership has to take a stand. When I mentioned that our service could be "mechanical," I was taking one comment out of a thousand but it was an important directional comment that supported the change we knew we had to make. It was no longer about doing what the "Joneses" did; it was about doing what the Joneses didn't do! But when it comes to change, if it is not obvious to everyone that change is required and there are no negative numbers to prompt the change—no burning bridge—then you absolutely need everyone to buy in or the change will not be successful. When you make a change to the bible, you've got to make sure the constituents have a big say in it.

The Ritz-Carlton hotel employees did have a big say in the changes. Senior leaders conducted dozens of focus groups and Cooper met personally with thousands of employees around the world to develop a new set of service values. Interestingly, most early objections came from the management ranks. They were concerned about losing the "mystique" that guests came to identify with the brand. According to Cooper, internal surveys found that only 30 percent of managers supported the changes while 90 percent of front-line employees believed they were necessary. Cooper repeated what he had heard from rank-and-file employees to overcome the objections of the management. Ultimately everyone got on board because they believed that listening to the people who created the experience for their guests would result in the right course of action.

Nobody Has an Emotional Experience with a Thing

In a service environment like the Ritz Carlton, the goal is to create an emotional engagement with the brand, a connection so strong that "A guest will not consider staying anywhere else and an employee would not think of making a career anywhere else," says Cooper.

"Mr. Cooper," I interrupted during our conversation, "At no point have I heard you mention anything about the beds, the furniture, the flat screen televisions, or the quality of the rooms. Don't they count in creating this experience?"

"The quality of our beds are the table legs for our industry," says Cooper. "In a luxury hotel, you would not expect to pull back the bed to find that the sheet is ripped, or someone has left clothes in the drawer, or the coffee is cold, or the elevator doesn't work, or TV doesn't work. You have got to provide a great sleep experience, spotlessly clean rooms, and a seamless process of checking people in. Those processes have to be in place. But once they are, an emotional engagement with our guests comes through the experience they have with our people. Nobody has an emotional experience with a thing."

The Ritz-Carlton began implementing twelve new service values in 2006. Each value starts with "I" because every employee plays a part in building the mystique. Some examples include "I am empowered to create unique, memorable, and personal experiences for our guests" (Service Value #3), "I understand my role in creating The Ritz-Carlton mystique" (Service Value #4), "I own and immediately resolve guest problems" (Service Value #6), and "I am involved in the planning of the work that affects me" (Service Value #9). *I am involved.* These three words in Service Value #9 hold the key behind the mystique; three words that separate exceptional service from a sloppy experience and unhappy customers. Invite your employees to participate in the creation of the brand. Listen to what they have to say. Take action on their feedback and watch them walk through walls for you.

Get 'Em to Care

The twelve values of The Ritz-Carlton are intended to create an "emotional engagement" between the brand and its guests. Engagement is a key to success when dealing with both customers and employees. Studies have shown that companies with highly engaged employees—those who are committed to the vision of the company—are more likely to have lower turnover and enjoy above-average productivity, profits, and customer loyalty. Griffin Hospital and The Ritz-Carlton certainly prove that this is true, but they are the exception. *HR Magazine* gathered the conclusions of several studies and found that "a fourth of employees are totally turned off by their jobs, fully half the workers do just enough to get by, and only the remaining 25 percent are enthusiastic."[6] In short, most workers in America today show up and go through the motions. They are not inspired to go the extra mile because they do not feel involved in the success of their organization. Here's what smart companies know: Asking for input and acting on it is a sure-fire way to improve engagement at all levels of the organization.

LISTENING TO GEN-X

Young people in business today crave feedback and interaction with their peers and managers—much more so than previous generations did. When researchers at Hudson, a professional staffing firm, conducted a survey of 2,000 employees, they found striking differences between generations in their attitudes toward their bosses and coworkers. One-quarter of Generation X (born between 1965 and 1979) and Generation Y (born after 1980) considered it very important to get feedback from their bosses at least once a week.[7] However, only 11 percent of "traditionalists" (born between 1928 and 1945) desired that level of communication. Generation Y employees also wanted greater social interaction with their managers. Young people want to be heard.

DIGG THIS: CONNECTING WITH PEOPLE WHO WANT CONNECTION

Every month, millions of people submit, share, or read news articles "dug up" and posted by members of the Web community Digg.com. The hugely popular site was cofounded by Jay Adelson, whom I interviewed for a Businessweek.com column. His company had recently been featured on the cover of the magazine. According to Adelson, members of Generation Y—the millennium generation—have high expectations of themselves and their colleagues. Members of this group want to work with highly engaged managers who help them grow and develop their professional skills.[8] Adelson argues that younger workers are transforming the workplace from the get-rich-quick attitude of the 1990s to a culture of empowerment and contribution. At the end of the day, he says, these employees want to feel as if they are part of something extraordinary and, more important, have contributed to its achievements.

Adelson says young people are asking themselves "Am I important? Am I offering value?" The key to managing this generation is to create excitement about the company's achievements and help employees recognize their own roles in accomplishing that mission. Empowering means soliciting employees' input and giving them a role in the decision-making process. Meetings, for example, should be more than a method of "broadcasting" a direction; they should be considered two-way communications, forums for asking other people to contribute their ideas and letting them know that their opinions are both welcome and valued.

Keeping Office Hours at Google

Google Vice President Marissa Mayer holds up to seventy meetings a week.[9] That does not leave a lot of time for unscheduled sessions where her team members just want to bounce an idea off of her for a few minutes. Mayer knows that her young colleagues want feedback—the more immediate the better—so she brought an idea to Google from her days teaching computer science at Stanford: For about ninety minutes a day, beginning

(continued)

at 4:00 p.m, she holds office hours. Employees add their names to a board outside her office, and she visits with them on a first-come, first-serve basis. Sometimes project managers need quick approval on a marketing campaign or engineers might want a few minutes to pitch a new design idea. According to Mayer, many of Google's most interesting products—such as Google News and Google Desktop—were first voiced in one of these informal meetings. During those ninety minutes at the end of the day, Mayer can have fifteen meetings. Those fifteen people may each have spent only five or six minutes with her, but they all leave knowing that they have been heard.

BE A MENTOR, NOT A TASKMASTER

Around the time I interviewed Adelson, I came across a Dilbert cartoon that showed Catbert—the evil director of HR—showing a new employee around the building. When Catbert introduced the wide-eyed worker to Alice, his new "mentor," she strangled him and screamed, "I don't have time to babysit! I'm buried in work! I do not like you!" That's a humorous extreme, of course, but it makes the point that many bosses spend more time controlling deadlines and delegating tasks and less time mentoring their subordinates. According to Adelson, managing is no longer just about hitting certain metrics; it's about understanding individuals and helping them grow. "Young people want a mentor, not a taskmaster," he says. He believes that 50 percent of a manager's time should be allocated to developing staff. That sounds like a lot to ask, but, Adelson reasons, "If managers aren't doing that, then the headcount is wrong, the budgeting process is wrong, or the company has tried to create too much efficiency. You'll burn people out."

For you as a supervisor, manager, or boss, understanding the goals of your younger employees requires that you ask questions and actually listen to their responses. An employee who wants to express herself creatively might not feel fulfilled inputting data into a spreadsheet, but how would you know that unless you had open conversations with her, asking her about her work, life, and career, and using these to help her reach her goals? A strong manager can be a mentor, generate respect among younger people, and also develop relationships with staff that foster trust and admiration from both sides. If an employee's goals are not in line with her job functions, then the job is wrong for the employee. It is the responsibility of the manager to help employees find the right roles where they have the best chance of success. If employees are engaged, the manager is getting the most out of the staff and the company is more productive.

Hear What People Have to Say

Leaders, entrepreneurs, and businesspeople at the top of their professions agree that a crucial component in engaging others is to listen. Once you place a high priority on listening, you will see a world of difference in the way you connect with your employees, customers, clients, or anyone else you come in contact with. Here is what extraordinary business professionals have to say on the subject:

> Good listening skills educate, motivate, help innovate, build business, nurture trust, and create a sense of inclusion. Bad listening skills, on the other hand, can lead to a world of pain.
> —Pat Croce, former president of the Philadelphia 76ers, in his book, *Lead or Get off the Pot!*[10]

> Most people overvalue talking and undervalue listening, even those in people-related jobs such as sales. But the truth is effective communication is not persuasion. It's listening . . . listen twice as much as you speak.
> —John Maxwell in *Becoming a Person of Influence*[11]

So many people in broadcasting, and indeed in life, love the sound of their own voice and don't listen to what the other person is saying.

The truest thing I've ever heard in my life is "I never learned anything when I was talking." If you apply this to your everyday life, in all areas of your life—personal and professional—you will be much richer in the long run. The key is to pay attention."

—Larry King, in *The Experts' Guide to 100 Things Everyone Should Know How to Do*[12]

Courage is what it takes to stand up and speak; courage is also what it takes to sit down and listen.

—Winston Churchill

LESSONS ON LISTENING

It should be clear by now that effective listening means more than keeping your mouth shut. Great listeners invite people into the process of creation, show genuine interest, and use the information they learn to improve the way they do business. Over the course of my career as a communications coach, I have listened to my clients and learned something from each and every one of them. Here are some tips I have picked up along the way:

Avoid interrupting. Let people have their say. Allow them to finish a thought before you speak. Most people spend the majority of a conversation either talking or thinking about what they will say next. Flip it around. Spend more time listening and less time thinking about what you will say when you get a chance to open your mouth.

Restate the information. My wife says that I "Google" her too often. I focus on only one or two words that she says, just as a Google search may zero in on only one or two words in your search phrase. For example, when she says, "Please go to the store for paper towels, milk, and two packages of blueberries,"

I may interpret her request as "Go to the store for blueberries." One technique for avoiding "Google" syndrome is to repeat back to the listener what he or she just said. In the instance with my wife, I would now say, "Paper towels, milk, and two packages of blueberries. Got it. If they don't have blueberries, would you prefer something else?"

Ditch the BlackBerry. I am not asking you to go cold turkey. There are not enough rehabilitation centers in Malibu to handle the influx of people who would be in need of detox. But for Pete's sake, turn it off during a meeting. Better yet, make a show of it and turn it off in front of your listener. During a workshop I led for a group of executives, one person spent the entire two hours punching out messages on her BlackBerry, glancing up from time to time. I cannot imagine how she must have made her employees feel. The same goes for sales professionals. Customers demand your undivided attention. It shows respect.

Fix your gaze. Remember what my reporter acquaintance said about his meeting with Bill Clinton? "His gaze never left my eyes." Maintaining eye contact with the person speaking to you is one of the easiest ways to make a connection and to convey that you care about what the person says. I know one business leader who some say is the most charismatic person they have ever met. When someone asks a question during a presentation, he walks closer to the employee and fixes his gaze on the person. He leans forward and nods as the question is being asked. Then he pauses briefly before answering to show how much thought he has given to the question. People say he makes them "feel important." How many times have you been speaking to someone only to see that person continuously look over your shoulder? Not very inspiring, is it? Listen with your body as well as your mind.

Be humble. Ralph Waldo Emerson once said, "Every man I meet is in some way my superior. In that, I learn of him." My wife worked for a division of a company filled with bright, passionate, and committed individuals who had a deep, thorough knowledge of their industry. A new manager stepped in and immediately hired an outside "consultant" before even asking for feedback from employees who had given their souls to the company for years. Employees were demoralized and uninspired. The division lost many good employees before the company realized the manager had to go. Leave your ego at the door, and learn from the front lines.

Acknowledge their pain. I remember working with a very charismatic salesman at a leading technology company that sells specialized software tools to engineers. The industry is very complex and arcane, so you can imagine how staff meetings must be. But I watched as this salesman gave a presentation to a group of potential new customers. He could have started by saying something really boring like "Our software tools are more effective at helping you design and simulate the performance of electronic circuits." The engineers in the audience would have understood that language, but the goal of this particular salesman was to "inspire" his listeners, engineers or not, by letting them know that he had listened to their concerns. He began by saying "I've spoken to many of you already and, from what I hear, you don't have time to waste. New technologies are making your work tougher than ever and more time consuming. You're creating chips that go into some really cool devices like the iPod, but you don't have time to enjoy those gadgets or spend time with your families! I think you'll be impressed at just how much time our new software tools will save you." This salesman inspires by selling the benefit (Simple Secret

#3), but he also grabs the attention and agreement of his audience by acknowledging their pain. His customers feel as if he listens to them and understands their needs.

Use five magic words. Studies show that simply asking for another's opinion significantly enhances your positive image of that individual. People want to talk about themselves and they want to know that they are being heard. After speaking to the leaders featured in this chapter, I have a new respect for these five simple words: "I would like your opinion." Managers at The Ritz-Carlton and Griffin have made conscious decisions to solicit opinions by constantly asking their employees how their businesses can be better. You do not have to be the CEO of a major brand to put these five words to use. A coach can use the five words to solicit input from bench players who might not feel that they're contributing to the success of the team; a saleswoman might use the five words to solicit input from her customers about how to improve her service. The listener will end up more inclined to support the supervisor, coach, or salesperson because they—the listener—have been *heard*.

As I have tried to reinforce in previous chapters, you cannot inspire people unless they like you, and they will like you if you ask for their feedback, genuinely listen to their opinions, and turn their suggestions into action. We all want to feel important, special, and included. Invite people in, make them feel better about themselves and their contributions, and watch your popularity skyrocket!

CHAPTER 6

Reinforce an Optimistic Outlook

Become a Beacon of Hope

> Optimism is an essential ingredient of innovation. How else can the individual welcome change over security, adventure over staying in safe places?
>
> —Robert Noyce, cofounder of Intel and co-inventor of the computer chip

Inspiring individuals are optimistic. Pessimists will beat themselves up for "losing" a sale. Optimists do not lose sales. A customer interaction might not have resulted in the intended outcome, but it did produce a result. Optimists will use the outcome to learn, adjust, and grow to have a better chance of success the next time. Their words and demeanor always reflect the confidence they maintain in themselves and their team.

USA Today sponsored a survey of 293,000 employees and found that "senior managers were more optimistic about almost everything at work.... Leaders, for some reason, see a bright future in the thickest fog."[1] Although the survey focused on the senior leadership ranks, the same can be said of inspiring individuals at every level. Certainly, as the leader of your personal brand, you must speak words of optimism, strength, and confidence if you hope to influence others to your way of thinking. As Marcus Buckingham observes in *The One Thing You Need to Know*, "The opposite of a leader isn't a follower. The opposite of a leader is a pessimist."[2] People who nail Simple Secret #6 always see a better tomorrow and help their colleagues, customers, or clients do the same. The words they choose reflect the world they see: one of hope, potential, and possibility.

Seeing a Bright Future in the Thickest Fog

After the attacks on the World Trade Center on September 11, 2001, online travel company Site59 was hit especially hard. Its headquarters sat next to a firehouse just two blocks from Ground Zero. The firehouse lost five men who were among the first to respond to the attacks. Site59's employees were understandably traumatized after seeing a tragedy of that magnitude literally unfold before their eyes, and returning to work only compounded their fears. Nobody was traveling; the company's revenue plummeted 70 percent, and employees feared that they would lose their jobs.

The company's founder Michelle Peluso told me that before her first meeting in Site59's temporary office space, she knew that she faced the most important discussion of her career.[3] Peluso's employees would either rally to create a better future or lose sight of the work they had to do to take care of themselves, the company, and their customers. According to Peluso, "I remember being very genuine and raw. I was profoundly affected by the events and I didn't hide it, but I also expressed the fierce, competitive, and angry spirit that we needed at the time. 'We do a great job for our customers and suppliers and will continue to do so. This will not be the end of us,' I told them. I reminded my employees that we were small, nimble, and fast-moving.

Given our size, we were in a unique position to innovate and rebound faster."

Peluso's words sparked a turnaround in perception. Everyone walked out of the room with a renewed sense of hope. "It was the most profound demonstration of how communication could make a group of people more committed and united," says Peluso. The team not only rallied but grew closer both professionally and personally. They even took turns cooking meals every Monday at the local firehouse. The company rebounded, continued to grow, and was purchased by Travelocity the next year. A short time later, Peluso was named Travelocity's President and Chief Executive Officer. Napoleon once said, "A leader is a dealer in hope." Peluso certainly fits that description. Her words revealed a human side that touched Peluso's colleagues on an emotional level and demonstrated strength, confidence, and optimism that would help them rise to meet an unprecedented challenge.

Few people in history have demonstrated more optimism in dark hours than Winston Churchill. In 1940 Nazi Germany unleashed a sustained bombing campaign on London. The blistering attack lasted for months and had two objectives: to destroy the Royal Air Force and to decimate the morale of Londoners. It did neither. In *We Shall Not Fail*, Churchill's granddaughter, Celia Sandys, says her grandfather saw reasons for hope and confidence during the gloomiest of times and, more important, succeeded in infusing that optimism in the people around him; people felt braver in his presence. "Churchill was blessed with an affirmative quality modern leaders admire. He exuded hope and confidence," Sandys writes.[4] "Inspirational leaders are beacons of hope. They project an aura of confidence and resolve that is quite literally contagious."[5]

Churchill had an unbreakable spirit, which he transmitted to others in his speaking. He acknowledged the hurdles to overcome, then shifted the focus to reasons for hope. According to Sandys, "Churchill's genius was to find a way to talk about bad news while finding hope in what others might see as defeat. He could put nearly any disaster in context. In October of 1940, after devastating air raids, Churchill gave a speech about how the cities 'would rise from their ruins' and blitzed homes would be rebuilt 'more to our credit than some of them were before.' Every leader could use Churchill's measured optimism. He saw the glass as half full, never half empty."[6]

When people are most likely to see defeat, you must radiate hope, confidence, and possibility. When members of Michelle Peluso's team could have allowed themselves to be consumed by the tragedy of September 11, Peluso validated their feelings and galvanized their collective strength at the same time. If she had failed to reinforce Site59's unique position in the industry, her employees and colleagues may have left the meeting demoralized instead of strengthened by her words. Always speak of a brighter future in the thickest fog.

Quite literally as I finished writing the last paragraph, I caught one of my clients, the chief financial officer of a large, publicly traded company in an interview on Bloomberg television. Its stock was down 10 percent after the company's quarterly earnings announcement, and her guidance for the year had caused concern among stock analysts, but she did not flinch from tough questions.

She acknowledged that times were tough for her company's entire industry, but she reminded viewers that her company had survived and thrived in similar conditions and, in fact, is now better positioned than its competitors to emerge even stronger when the economy improves. This CFO was poised, confident, and self-assured. The stock rebounded nicely by the end of the day, mostly due to the her words of reassurance. She answered tough questions with a sense of hope and optimism. The numbers themselves looked bad, and it was up to her to put them in perspective; she accomplished it beautifully, and the company could get back to the task of creating products that will continue to improve the lives of millions of its customers.

Every day we are presented with opportunities to inspire our investors, customers, colleagues, peers, family, and friends. Speak optimistically. Give people a reason for hope.

A Formula for Success

"Be an optimist and a dreamer. Expect greatness from yourself, and the best kind of unexpected surprises will find their way into your life."

—Mark Burnett, Jump In![7]

Unshakable Optimism

The positive psychology movement has taught us that thinking optimistically has a dramatic effect on our moods. Being in a good mood will raise your energy, give power to your words, and boost your professional presence. Talking to yourself in optimistic language releases powerful endorphins—feel-good chemicals—in your brain. Endorphins also flood our brains when we excel at a particular task or someone says something that boosts our self-esteem. Do you see the connection? The link between optimism and inspiration is direct and immediate: *Thinking* optimistically will make you feel better about yourself. *Speaking* optimistically will give others the confidence to follow your vision.

Every person I interviewed for this book speaks with unshakable optimism. Their confidence in their vision is overwhelming: Ritz-Carlton president Simon Cooper was confident he could create a customer service culture that would be unmatched in his industry. Cranium founder Richard Tait was confident he could create a board game that would rival anything sold by the behemoths of the toy industry:

Mattel and Hasbro. 24 Hour Fitness founder Mark Mastrov was confident that he could turn his small gym in San Leandro, California, into a worldwide chain of health clubs. Disney teacher of the year Ron Clark was confident he could take a class of underachieving school kids in Harlem and motivate them to outperform the "gifted" children by the end of the year. There's a pattern. As General Colin Powell has said, "Optimism is a 'force multiplier.'"[8] Nothing is as powerful as an optimistic attitude in motivating yourself and the people around you.

Optimism as a Survival Strategy

I once heard a story about a military trainer for the Special Forces who said that if he had to choose between two people he could be lost with in the jungle—one who has survival skills and no confidence, the other who has no survival skills but all the confidence in the world—he would prefer to join the confident one; the optimistic person would stand a better chance of getting out of the jungle alive. In the corporate jungle, who would you rather have by your side: the person who sees the gloom in everything or the one with an unshakable belief in his ability to find a solution? Be the person people want to join.

FIVE STEPS TO OPTIMISM

Optimism can be learned. Psychologists are discovering that, to a large extent, our attitudes are handed down by our parents. This means that you can change. I believe a big part of our growth cycle requires us to build on the qualities handed down by our parents: Embrace their positive qualities and learn from their weaknesses. I hope that my daughters, Josephine and Lela, adopt my best qualities and improve on my weaker ones (few as they may be!). Life is growth. Grow stronger by building on the foundation set by your parents; if the foundation is shaky, here are five steps for developing optimistic habits that will turn you into an inspirational role model for everyone you encounter.

Step 1. Build on Your Strengths.   Inspiring communicators focus on their achievements; they learn from setbacks but never consider them "failures." Events that most of us might perceive as catastrophic are just temporary blips in the eyes of these individuals. Think about it this way: Successful baseball players would have almost no chance of making contact with the ball if they focused only on their strikeouts. A baseball player who lacks confidence at the plate is doomed. Even the best players in the league strike out more often than they make a hit. Great players use their strikeouts as learning opportunities, and build on their strengths.

In fact, innovative companies actually encourage people to fail. Google recommends that its engineers carve out 20 percent of their time to dream up new ideas. Seriously. When engineers are given room to fail, they actually increase their chances for success. I heard that Google expects its engineers to "fail" at 70 percent of the projects that they are encouraged to dream up. It's the other 30 percent that turn into successful ideas, and these home runs have turned Google into an Internet powerhouse.

Like baseball players and Google innovators, computer chip engineers "fail" far more often than they succeed. Robert Noyce coinvented the integrated circuit—the component that computer chips are made of—and started Intel to produce and manufacture his invention. Noyce never would have succeeded if he had not built on his successes and discarded his mistakes. "Don't be encumbered by history," Noyce was once quoted as saying. "Go off and do something wonderful." My clients at Intel who worked with Noyce remember him as "optimistic," "charismatic," and "admired." Yes, admired. Notice how those three terms are used together. It starts with optimism. Optimistic people have more charisma. Charismatic people elicit more admiration from their team. It's a simple formula; follow it!

Step 2. Radiate Optimism. I remember my first day at a particular job. I was dressed nicely, but nothing too formal: black slacks, a dress shirt, and a sports jacket. I bumped into a woman in the elevator who had a frown on her face.

"First day?" she asked.

"Yes." I smiled as I extended a hand.

"You'll lose that jacket by tomorrow," she said. "And that smile will be off your face by the end of the day."

I thought I had walked into a Dilbert cartoon. What a downer! Within a few months this woman had been let go, and I was still showing up to work in slacks, a jacket, and a smile. The woman sucked the energy right out of a room; she couldn't have lasted long.

Years later, when I covered the Arnold Schwarzenegger administration for CBS, a staff member told me, "He [Arnold] makes me want to be a better person."

"Why?" I asked. "Because of what he has accomplished? His money? His fame? His biceps? What is it about the man that inspires you to be a better person?"

"He does not allow negativity. He does not flinch from the hard facts of a situation, and he always wants to tackle the tough issues with as much information as possible, but he demands that the conversation focus on finding solutions and not on raising more obstacles. Negatives are a no-no."

Schwarzenegger knows that to be an action hero in real life, his demeanor must be positive, confident, and optimistic. He carries himself like a man of action. He stands tall, walks briskly, shakes hands with gusto, and maintains eye contact with his listeners. A discussion of the outward expression of confidence would be incomplete without touching on body language. Your words are important, but what your body says before you say a word is equally vital, and aside from obvious body language like posture and a purposeful walk, there is one quality that will improve your body language tenfold immediately. Remember the newspaper reporter in Chapter 5 who said President Bill Clinton made him feel like the most important person in the room? Do you remember why? "His gaze never left my eyes," the reporter said. Make eye contact and keep it; you will seem confident and truly connect with others.

> Psychologists have discovered that if we show signs of confidence on the outside, we will feel confident on the inside as well. *Men's Health* magazine tackled the subject of nonverbal attraction in one issue. "As Paul Ekman, a famed researcher into nonverbal communication, showed in his experiments, if you spend enough time frowning, you'll begin to feel sad. If you stand up straight and walk with purpose, you'll feel more confident."[9] Smile and walk with purpose!

Step 3. Speak Highly of Yourself, Especially When Talking to Yourself!. When Norman Vincent Peale wrote *The Power of Positive Thinking*, he couldn't have known that a sports marvel by the name of Tiger Woods would take a positive mental attitude to the *n*th degree. "The road to failure is paved with negativity," Woods writes in *How I Play Golf.*[10] "If you think you can't do something, chances are you won't be able to. Conversely, the power of positive thinking can turn an adverse situation into a prime opportunity for heroism." Woods has a total and complete belief in himself and his skill. Some would argue that much of Woods's success is based on natural ability—he climbed out of his highchair and almost immediately struck a ball perfectly—his father's coaching, and his own disciplined commitment to never-ending improvement. It all counts, but it's the mental game that gives Woods an extra edge.

It is no coincidence that Woods's golf idol is Jack Nicklaus, another proponent of positive thinking. In an article for *Golf Digest*, famed sports psychologist Bob Rotella recounted a story about a fundraising dinner he and Nicklaus both attended.[11] During a talk, Nicklaus said he had never three-putted the last hole of a tournament or failed to sink it within five feet. Some members of the audience were puzzled. "Of course he had..." they thought. One person could not stand it any longer and called Nicklaus on it, but Nicklaus stood his ground.

Rotella made a brilliant observation about the incident. A 16-handicapper would replay the missed putt endlessly in his mind, but Nicklaus does not think like a 16-handicapper. He only remembers the putts he made. In his mind, he had never missed a short putt on a last hole!

Step 4. Surround Yourself with Builders, Not Detractors. A famous psychologist by the name of Lev Vygotsky was the first to coin the term "Zone of Proximal Development." My wife, who has a master's degree in psychology, first told me about it. The Zone of Proximal Development is known in child development circles as the difference between the child's current level of learning and the child's potential level of development. Bridging the gap is most often associated with the child's social interactions with peers and parents.[12] To me, it simply means that you are only as good as the people you hang with. Oprah Winfrey has said, "Surround yourself only with people who are going to lift you higher."[13] The rate of progress is based on how much positive outside influence we get from teachers, peers, and parents.

Writing a book like this is not easy. It requires countless hours with people who are very busy and difficult to track down, but I do it because these men and women have a lot to teach us. You are more likely to be extraordinary if you spend time with extraordinary people. Expose yourself to those who are wealthier, wiser, smarter, or better than you in one way or another. Learn from others and your communication will be more inspiring; listeners will be enchanted by how much they can learn from you.

Step 5. Create Magnificent Obsessions. Inspiring individuals dream bigger than everyone else. Their lives are spent in the pursuit of "magnificent obsessions," as motivational guru Tony Robbins has said. "Most people's goals are to 'pay their lousy bills,' to get by, to survive, to make it through the day—in short, they are caught up in the trap of making a living rather than designing a life," he writes in *Awaken the Giant Within*. "If we want to discover the unlimited possibilities within us, we must find a goal big enough and grand enough to challenge us to push beyond our limits and discover our true potential."

Donald Trump says if you're going to think, you might as well THINK BIG, and Starbucks founder Howard Schultz echoes this sentiment: If you're going to dream, you might as well DREAM BIG. Schultz did not plan to build a small chain of coffee bars in Seattle. He passionately believed Starbucks would eventually be a global brand, and so now it is. Both Trump and Schultz have magnificent obsessions, as does Cold Stone chief executive officer Doug Ducey, whom we met in Chapter 2.

As you might recall, in 1999 Ducey outlined a bold vision to significantly expand the number of Cold Stone franchises in a five-year time period. Some franchise owners considered it unimaginable, but in a conversation with Ducey, I learned that his goal of hitting 1,000 stores—although ambitious—was based on the success of Cold Stone's locations at the time.[15] Ducey's team looked closely at growth, customer feedback, return visits to existing stores, potential sites, interest from potential franchise owners, and other metrics before announcing the new vision. Ducey's vision was a big, hairy, audacious goal by anyone's standards, but do it they did. Ducey had created a magnificent obsession that rallied people around his vision.

Cold Stone's growth spurt began with a leader daring to dream bigger than everyone else, but this also holds true for the people you influence in your personal life. My goddaughter, Nicole, graduated from a small-town high school where a very small percentage of her peers decided to continue their education at a four-year college. Few of these students were ever given the information or drive they needed to dream of a better life.

But my wife and I had big dreams for Nicole. We had constant and consistent conversations with her about college, and we made it more vivid by taking her on road trips so that she could feel and see herself on a campus. The talks and trips worked, and although some of Nicole's friends were skeptical when she applied to several of the nation's most prestigious colleges, they became believers when a top-twenty university came knocking. This did not surprise me; what did surprise me was that her peers and even some teachers were stunned. They had never dreamed of these possibilities for Nicole. Sometimes people need help to blow beyond the perceived limitations that they—and others around them—have set for themselves.

As a speaker and coach, I meet new people all the time, and I am endlessly fascinated by the ones who stand apart and leave a positive impression on me; they are more optimistic than the rest. Their confidence in a better future is so strong that it makes me feel stronger in my own ability to contribute. Can this optimism be learned? Using the five steps I've just given, I believe it can.

Want to Be Loved? Be an Optimist

President Ronald Reagan passed away some fifteen years after he left the White House, yet the image of optimism he had radiated throughout

A former Fortune 500 executive, Bob Levinson raises millions of dollars for Lynn University in Boca Raton, Florida, in his current role as a fundraiser. His past and present success is not what makes him extraordinary; his outlook does. Levinson is one of the most enthusiastic and optimistic men I have ever met. But get this: Levinson has more energy and passion for his work than most thirty-something professionals do—and he is eighty-two years old. "A successful person has to have a sense of excitement and a positive mental attitude," he says.[16] "If you are excited, it will set the pace for everyone else in the organization." Levinson believes that we get out of bed and face two choices: to be grumpy and miserable, or to be excited and fired up. Here are Levinson's eight tips for starting the day ready to light up the world:

1. Read the death notices and think about how lucky you are to not be there!
2. Think of all the things you want to do and realize that the clock is ticking and you have a short time to accomplish them.
3. Look at those dear to you and think about how you are going to share in their future life.
4. Listen to good music when you get up in the morning to get your motor going.
5. Exercise every morning when you get up to get your juices flowing.
6. Always plan more than you can finish in a given day so that you cannot wait to start the next one.
7. Laugh a lot and try to be an exciting person.
8. Forget "too old"—or "too young"—and go for it!

Here's the point: Levinson makes a choice to live with a sense of hope, confidence, and optimism about the future, and it all starts with how he begins every day.

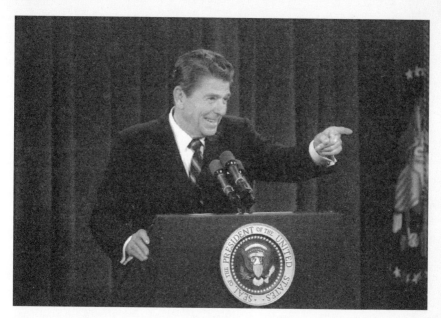

Figure 6.1 Optimism was the key to Reagan's charisma. (Photo C2476-24, "President Reagan giving a Press Conference in Room 450 of the Old Executive Office Building," June 16, 1981.
Courtesy of the Ronald Reagan Library, Simi Valley, California.

his lifetime moved people around the world on his death. In June of 2004 thousands of people lined the streets in Southern California as a procession brought the former President to his final resting place in Simi Valley. I watched as the cable news called the crowds "amazing" and "unbelievable." They were surprised at the outpouring of emotion for the great man; however, I fully expected it. Optimism had been Reagan's secret. (See Figure 6.1.)

Although most of Reagan's speeches were full of hope and confidence, I consider his final letter to the nation to be the best demonstration of this quality. Facing a life with Alzheimer's, which he knew would eventually cause him to forget that he had ever sat in the Oval office, Reagan wrote, "When the Lord calls me home, whenever that may be, I will leave with the greatest love for this country of ours and eternal optimism for its future. I now begin the journey that will lead me into the sunset of my life. I know that for America there will always be a bright new dawn ahead."[17] Optimism was the key to Reagan's charisma. His unshakable belief in brighter days ahead made people feel better about themselves and their country.

After Reagan's passing, General Colin Powell appeared on CNN. Powell had served as chairman of the Joint Chiefs of Staff during the Reagan administration. Speaking to Wolf Blitzer, Powell told a story about a period of time during his tenure when many people expressed concern about the U.S buying binge of wealthy Japanese businesspeople during the 1980s. Sarah Jessica Parker may want her "Jimmy Choos" on *Sex and the City* now, but in the 1980s Japanese investors wanted everything else, including American companies, real estate, and golf courses. (Pebble Beach was owned by the Japanese for a brief period of time.) When the federal administration asked Reagan what it should do about Japanese investment, according to Powell, Reagan just smiled and said that he was proud that the Japanese considered America to be such a great investment. His optimism "blew them away," said Powell.[18]

Blow them away. Make people feel better about you, themselves, and the organization in which they are placing their trust. Peddle hope and possibility.

Make Waves

The ripple effect of a leader's enthusiasm and optimism is awesome. So is the impact of cynicism and pessimism. Leaders who whine and blame engender those same behaviors among their colleagues.... Spare me the grim litany of the realist. Give me the unrealistic aspirations of the optimist any day.

—General Colin Powell, *Selling Power*[19]

Oprah Winfrey is another personality whose mind-blowing optimism should be a model for the rest of us; she speaks words of strength, hope, and confidence. On September 27, 2006, Oprah gave a speech to a women's business development group in Chicago, in which she spoke about her journey from the small town of Kosciusko, Mississippi, to where she stands today as one of the most influential people on the planet. She told of a recent trip to her hometown, when she built a Boys and Girls club. On the trip, she saw people she once knew sitting on the same porch steps. "It's like time stopped and continues to stand still; there's not a day I'm not on my knees thanking God that I was one of the blessed ones to be able to leave that place and do something with my life," Oprah said.[20]

Oprah understood that in order to grow, she had to get out of Dodge, both physically and mentally. Her life would not be a cakewalk; in the course of her career she faced racist news directors, dimwits (such as the man who told her to change her name to "Susie"), and skeptics who said she would never make it as a talk show host in Chicago. But Oprah dreamed bigger dreams and followed her passion to speak to the world "in a way that not only entertains, but uplifts and encourages and enlightens people."[21] Her plan was to speak words of inspiration and to use the power of communication to help others reach their potential. "Your work, your business, is your art. It is your art, it is your voice to the world. How you choose to use it either lifts the consciousness of the world or does not. And so I would say for everyone in here, hold on to your dreams. Believe in them because you only become what you believe."[22] Oprah has a voice that now reaches 23 million viewers a day who are inspired by her optimism. We all have a voice and a choice; we can choose to use that voice to tear others down and impose obstacles in their paths, or to encourage and uplift our listeners. The choice is up to you.

CHAPTER 7

Encourage Their Potential

Praise People, Invest in Them, and Unleash Their Potential

You can change the world by changing your words.
— Joel Osteen

My baby daughter Josephine is playing with her favorite toy—a 99-cent funnel from Wal-Mart. It's not something we bought her. During a staff meeting, my wife's former boss gave her the funnel to celebrate a particular accomplishment. She had completed a huge project with a tight deadline: She had taken a pile of information and "funneled" it into a concise document. The manager's heart was in the right place, but the way he recognized her left her uninspired. You see, the manager also took the opportunity to recognize everyone else in the department with cheap items like body spray for one appearance-conscious young man.

"Would you have been happier with an iPod?" I asked my wife.

"The funnel is not the point," she said. "If you're going to recognize me, praise me in front of my colleagues and single me out. Acknowledging everyone at the same time doesn't make me feel special."

My wife's observation hits on something that lies at the heart of inspiration. Since she is internally motivated to do the very best job

148

she can, she simply smiled, thanked her boss, shrugged it off, and went back to work. No harm done, right? *Wrong*. Because her boss had failed over time to encourage and praise her effectively when she did exemplary work, she was never inspired. So what did she do as soon as she had the chance? You got it: She left. The company lost an outstanding employee whom its clients adored.

You might recall what I said in the introduction about being the one who must motivate the people around you. Inspiring individuals in any field have mastered Simple Secret #7: They encourage people to reach their potential by effectively praising them, emotionally investing in them, and helping them to unleash their talents.

If you live in a perpetual state of "gimme, gimme, gimme," you will end up with far less than you deserve. Building people up and helping them reach their fullest potential as human beings will bring far more pleasure than you could ever imagine. In our society, we often strive for the trappings of success: monster homes, cars, yachts, and assorted "bling." My wife and I were invited to an exclusive dinner in Las Vegas one night. The couple at the table obviously had more money than they knew what to do with. The husband told me his watch cost $50,000 and only twenty had been made. He told me that some rapper had one, a guy named 50 Cent. I called him Nickel for the longest time until my wife corrected me. I could have cared less, but it meant the world to that man. Yes, some people like the bling. It makes them feel important.

But for most of us, our dearest treasures are people: family and friends, spouses and kids, parents and grandparents. People connect with people, not things. And the best compliment you can receive from another human being is this: "You make me want to be a better person."

Pastor and best-selling author Joel Osteen says, "As parents, we can profoundly influence the direction of our children's lives by the words we say to them. I believe as husbands and wives we can set the direction for our entire family. As a business owner, you can help set the direction of your employees. With our words, we have the ability to help mold and shape the future of anyone over whom we have influence."[1] At work or at home, the words we choose and the stories we tell have the power to inspire people or break them down. Of course, you don't have to be a pastor to speak words of encouragement, but as an evangelist for your own brand, lifting people's spirits will gain their respect, admiration, and loyalty.

Satisfy a Basic Human Need

Sincere praise is the easiest way to connect with another human being. According to *Don't Sweat the Small Stuff* author Richard Carlson, "Shower your co-workers with genuine, well-deserved compliments.... In all the years I've been studying human behavior and attitude, I've heard hundreds of employees say they feel underappreciated, but I've never heard a single one say they feel overappreciated. This strategy speaks for itself."[2] Your job as a motivator is to make people feel good about themselves and boost their self-esteem, confidence, and courage.

When people receive genuine praise, their doubt diminishes and their spirits soar. After my coaching sessions, my goal is to leave clients feeling more confident than they were at the start. They need to be bold to tackle speaking events that can make or break their reputation or that of their company. I'm tough on them; we often only have a short time to work, so they will hear comments from me that their colleagues might feel uncomfortable making. Regardless of their position or net worth, though, they need praise as much as the next person. It's a human craving.

Why then do most people fail to supply this most basic of human emotions? The answer is in the funnel story at the beginning of this chapter. Most people have a good heart but lack the tools to make praise effective; your praise must be local, frequent, and constructive.

GIVE PEOPLE THEIR FIFTEEN MINUTES

Today there are about seventy-five reality shows on major television networks. Millions of viewers cannot turn away from watching people trying to make it as singers, dancers, chefs, rock stars, and the like. Everyone, it seems, wants fifteen minutes of fame. Understanding this will help you inspire others. If people want to be famous, let them. You may not be able to give people shots at superstardom, but do not underestimate the power of stardom in their own environments.

According to *Freakonomics* coauthor Stephen J. Dubner, "One mistake a lot of people make when creating incentive schemes is thinking that financial incentives are the most powerful incentive going. In fact, social and moral incentives are often more powerful. The other thing to consider is what I sometimes call 'local fame;' very few of us want to be (or will ever be) truly famous. What we want is to be famous 'locally,' if even for a short time—that is, known well among our peers, families, friends, etc., for having done something well and noteworthy."[3]

Recall The Ritz-Carlton "wow" stories in Chapter 4: Each story praises the efforts of one individual who provided a memorable and unique experience for a hotel guest. Praising one individual serves two purposes: It reinforces one of the twelve core values of the organization and it recognizes that individual in front of his or her peers. The person receives "local" fame, in front of a dozen or more colleagues at his or her hotel, and worldwide fame at the corporate level, when the story is shared among the 35,000 hotel employees of The Ritz-Carlton in twenty-one countries.

FILLING EMOTIONAL TANKS

Jim Thompson is the executive director of the Positive Coaching Alliance, a nonprofit organization that has sparked a movement of 200,000 youth sports coaches, training in the group's mission: to use sports to teach character. "Double-Goal" coaches are those who want to win but also aim to teach life lessons through sports. According to Thompson, there are infinite teachable moments in youth sports that are overlooked by coaches and parents who are obsessed with winning.[4] For example, if a kid strikes out, a "First-Goal" coach might have a conversation with the player about improving her mechanics. A "Double-Goal" coach covers the mechanics, but also uses the moment to teach traits like resilience, bouncing back from setbacks, and giving it your best shot.

Effective praise is a key component of the Positive Coaching program. According to Thompson, the secret to effective praise is the "Magic 5:1 Ratio"—find five reasons to praise for every one thing to criticize. Thompson calls it filling a person's emotional tank:

> We all have emotional tanks like a gas tank in a car. If it's empty, your car doesn't run. If it's low, you're not going to perform well. You can get people to do something out of fear for a short term. But the very best coaches build up their athletes or employees so they are excited and can't wait to go to work and face the challenge. Constant criticism drains tanks. We're not anti-criticism but you need to offer receivable criticism. I may be right in my criticism, but if I'm draining their tank while I'm doing it, they may spend internal emotional energy resisting, arguing and not embracing the criticism. Give receivable feedback.

Note: Thompson has not only articulated a vivid vision of a better future (Simple Secret #2), but he also sells benefits for players and parents (Simple Secret #3) and uses examples, stories, metaphors, and other rhetorical techniques (Simple Secret #4).

BETTER THAN PEANUT BUTTER AND JELLY

Thompson suggests that praise is most effective when included in a "criticism sandwich." In one scenario, a young basketball player keeps missing three-point shots due to a lack of follow-through. A criticism sandwich would begin with praising something the player is doing right. For example, "I like the way you bend your knees, that's where you are getting your power." The praise could be followed by a constructive criticism, intended to help the player improve in a specific area: "If you remember to follow through—do the gooseneck—you'll make more shots." This would then be followed up with more praise, like a sandwich: "I also like the way you keep your eye on the basket after you've thrown the ball." The player gets three coaching lessons, with the criticism sandwiched between two praises. It fills the player's emotional tank.

Before embarking on his path to bring character back to sports, Thompson taught global management courses at the Stanford Graduate School of Business. He believes that the Positive Coaching model holds value for business professionals as well, and uses the criticism sandwich with his own staff. Each staff meeting at Positive Coaching Alliance begins with fifteen minutes of "Appreciations and Triumphs." This presents an opportunity for employees to publicly recognize someone else in the meeting. One person might acknowledge a colleague who stayed late to help assemble material for a project or for making a special trip over a weekend for a pitch. Public recognition makes people feel good about the company and each other. According to Thompson, "If we have difficult decisions to make, we can solve problems much more effectively because everyone's emotional tanks are full."

Thompson believes the average person feels underappreciated, and surveys of workplace morale agree. Most people work hard but do not feel acknowledged, which leaves them demoralized and fed up. "But in an environment where people are noticed for good things—or even for taking their best shot if they fail—they're more likely to be fired up!" says Thompson. A great coach can turn an athlete with a lot of heart and a little skill into a standout. Michael Jordan didn't win a championship until Phil Jackson came along (who, by the way, is a proponent for the Positive Coaching program and serves as its national spokesperson) and helped Jordan become a champion (six times!). See yourself as a "Double-Goal" coach in your business relationships: Help your employees and colleagues master "the mechanics"—the nuts and bolts of their job—while encouraging them to reach their potential as champions in and out of the office.

Act Like a Virgin

My approach to being a good boss is not different from being a good father.... If you lavish praise, people will flourish. If you criticize people, they will shrivel up.
—Virgin entrepreneur Richard Branson[5]

Make an Emotional Investment in People

Mark Mastrov turned his passion for fitness into profit—a big profit. Nearly 25 years ago, Mastrov received a $20 Christmas bonus as a salesman for health-food products. Disappointed, he decided to go into business for himself. Investing $15,000 he borrowed from his grandmother, Mastrov became co-owner of a gym near San Francisco, California. Over the next two decades, it grew into a worldwide chain of health clubs, some of which are in partnerships with sports celebrities like Magic Johnson, Lance Armstrong, and Andre Agassi. Today, 3 million fitness buffs enjoy the amenities offered at more than 400 24 Hour Fitness clubs around the world, and the chain recently was sold to private equity firm Forstmann Little for $1.6 billion. Still very much involved, Mastrov travels the globe as 24 Hour's chairman. (See Figure 7.1.)

Figure 7.1 24 Hour Fitness founder Mark Mastrov encourages big dreams. Photo by Paul Body, www.paulbodyphoto.com, "Mark Mastrov and Shaq," 2006. Courtesy of 24 Hour Fitness.

More than 21,000 sales associates work in Mastrov's clubs, and most of them would walk through walls for him and their immediate supervisors. Mastrov makes an emotional investment in his people and expects his managers to do the same. That means caring about people as individuals and showing genuine concern for their families, interests, and goals. This quality is most important in reaching Gen Xers, according to Mastrov. "Sales associates are younger people looking for leaders who they believe in and want to follow. Managers should sit down with them and ask what their goals and aspirations are. Ask them what they want in life and how working for 24 Hour Fitness will help achieve those goals. Ask them about their family and friends, their passions and interests. Bring up those questions even before you ask how sales are going. It shows that you care about who they are. It earns respect and it's the easiest thing to do!"[6]

When Mastrov walks away from a sales associate, he wants that person to feel uplifted and inspired. He remembers important dates, birthdays, or events and the names of kids or spouses; it shows that he genuinely cares about them as human beings. "I can always bring up business, but they need to see that I care about them first," Mastrov says. Motivating is about bringing out the best in people, but people will not listen to your message until they know you care. Show that you care about them personally, and you will bring out their best professionally.

Unleash Their Talents

In between *Friends* and *Studio 60 on the Sunset Strip,* actor Matthew Perry starred in a made-for-TV movie about one of the most inspiring teachers in America: Ron Clark. In 2000 Clark was named Disney's American Teacher of the Year and wrote a best-selling book about his "rules" for motivating students, *The Essential 55.*

Clark was teaching elementary school in North Carolina when he heard about a Harlem school that was having difficulty attracting first-rate teachers. He went to the school and began teaching fifth grade. There he accomplished something truly extraordinary. Clark told me that when he took over the class, none of the kids were performing at grade level in either math or reading, but by the end of the school year, the class had outperformed even the "gifted" class on their test scores![7] Fast forward to today: Every one of the students from Clark's fifth-grade Harlem class are in high school; not one has dropped out, despite the area's high dropout rate.

Although Clark brought a number of innovative teaching techniques to his class, he says the secret to inspiring students (and adults) is to help them unleash their talents by showing them that you genuinely believe in their ability to succeed. "As a leader, you must set the tone. When you walk into a classroom or boardroom you need to lift everyone up, to applaud them, to believe in them, to set high expectations, and do whatever it takes to help them meet the goal. I have worked with kids who had low self-esteem and test scores. But I believed in them. That's a powerful emotion. I walked in and saw a world for those kids. I put fire in that classroom because I believed in them."

Bring out the best in people by believing only the best about them. Clark's class would have not stood a chance if he had accepted the conventional belief that his students would be lucky to score at their grade level. The administrators even asked Clark if he wanted to teach the "gifted" students. Clark would have none of it. Ron Clark's optimism (Simple Secret #6) made him incapable of accepting failure for the kids he sought to motivate. The words he used with his students always reflected his belief in them. The kids had been torn down all their lives, but Clark's message built them up, and they believed in him because he made them believe in themselves. The people who believe in themselves the least need inspiration the most.

Your Ultimate Inspiration

Watching others succeed motivates inspiring leaders. During one of our conversations, Travelocity CEO Michelle Peluso said, "There is nothing that gives me more of a sense of reward than watching our team performing at its highest level and seeing our people passionate and excited about our mission. If you were to ask me when I feel the happiest, I'd tell you it's when others are succeeding. It is really profound to watch someone succeed who I mentored or watched grow to take on more responsibility. Watching people succeed is a much more rewarding feeling that some of the other rewards you get as a CEO."[8]

I began this chapter with a quote by Pastor Joel Osteen: "You can change the world by changing your words." This also applies to your daily interactions, at work or at home. Use your words to bring out the best in your children, spouse, colleagues, and clients. They should feel better about themselves having been in your presence. Osteen has said we bring out the best in people by sowing seeds of encouragement; that means recognizing the greatness people have within them and helping them to see it themselves.

On September 5, 2005, Apple CEO Steve Jobs gave a stirring commencement speech to the graduating class of Stanford University. "Your time is limited, so don't waste it living someone else's life," he said.[9] "Don't be trapped by dogma, which is living with the results of other people's thinking. Don't let the noise of others' opinions drown out your own inner voice. And most importantly, have the courage to follow your heart and intuition. They somehow already know what you truly want to become." Don't ever place limitations on the dreams you have for yourself as a leader and communicator. You have the potential to positively influence everyone in your personal and professional life, but only if you speak words that lift the spirits of the people around you and encourage them to be their best selves.

Garth Brooks once dedicated a song to his mother with the lyrics "It was your song that made me sing, it was your voice that gave me wings, and it was your light that shined, guiding my heart to find this place where I belong."[10] Be the voice that guides others. Believe in people, encourage their potential, and inspire them to live the best life possible.

PART II

Living the
7 Simple Secrets

Inspire Every Day, in Every Office and in Every Home

More than two dozen extraordinary men and women have participated in the development of these techniques. You've met most of them in Part I. In Part II, you will meet more inspiring individuals through observations and conversations. Their insights demonstrate that inspiration takes place every day, in every office, and in every home. A brief conversation or a simple presentation offers the opportunity to inspire others to embrace your idea.

Before we launch into Part II, let's review the 7 Simple Secrets to firing up your listeners. INSPIRE stands for:

1. Ignite Your Enthusiasm
2. Navigate the Way
3. Sell the Benefit
4. Paint a Picture
5. Invite Participation
6. Reinforce an Optimistic Outlook
7. Encourage People to Reach Their Potential

The first seven chapters introduced the model; the seven chapters in Part II show you how people in a variety of roles apply it. Some of the featured individuals make millions of dollars; others make a decent salary but can't afford a private island just yet. Some run giant companies; others are well on their way to running companies of their own. Some are entrepreneurs; others are managers. And one even had a Hollywood movie made about his life. Here are exceptional individuals you'll meet:

- An IT manager for the U.S. Navy who motivates his crew members to perform their roles with exceptional professionalism
- A hotel supervisor who transforms ordinary staff meetings into opportunities to teach five-star service
- An award-winning public relations professional whose enthusiasm, passion, and insight wins over the hearts and minds of new business prospects
- A larger-than-life entrepreneur considered the most charismatic pitchman in the world
- A leader whose vision helped to transform a small chain of stores into one of the hottest franchises in America today
- A CEO who inspired his employees to attain a goal most thought was a mission impossible
- A teacher whose motivational techniques were so effective, a television movie was made about him

None of the accomplishments you will read about could have been possible without the inspiring communications skills introduced in Part I. In each chapter of Part II, one of the exceptional individuals, or "fire starters," just described will be featured. In each chapter, you will also find:

- The featured Fire Starter's role and key opportunity in that role
- A brief description of the featured Fire Starter

▌ Detailed descriptions for how the featured Fire Starter utilizes most or all of the 7 Simple Secrets

The descriptions present ideas and insights into how you can incorporate the Simple Secrets into your daily exchanges with employees, prospects, customers, investors, colleagues, students, or franchise owners. Start living the 7 Simple Secrets today!

CHAPTER 8

HOO-YAH! Optimism Rules aboard the USS *Ronald Reagan*

Fire Starter: Robert Labrenz
Role: IT Manager for the U.S. Navy
Opportunity: Motivate 75 junior crew members to perform their highly specialized jobs with professionalism, passion, and a commitment to excellence

Robert Labrenz is an officer and information technology (IT) instructor for the U.S. Navy. By the time you read this, Labrenz will be on a four-year tour of duty aboard the USS *Ronald Reagan*, the largest and most technically advanced aircraft carrier sailing the world's oceans. (The ship is powered by two nuclear reactors and is as long as the Empire State Building is tall.) Labrenz will lead a team of up to 75 technical specialists who support Web, e-mail, data centers, and PC hardware for the *Reagan's* 5,000-member crew. Labrenz is a manager who acts as a go-between the techs and senior command. He describes the job as "combat computing" because the planes don't fly without him![1] Labrenz contacted me after reading my first book and applying its presentation techniques to give him an edge over his peers. In February 2007 we discussed the 7 Simple Secrets model of inspiration and how it applies to an IT manager serving on a state-of-the-art carrier. Take note of how each and every one of the 7 Simple Secrets applies to his role as an IT manager aboard the USS *Ronald Reagan*.

Motivation plays an important role in the function of an IT department. From the moment Labrenz steps on a ship, all eyes are on him. He is recognized as a technical expert and expected to give sound, unwavering advice that requires respect. According to Labrenz, "If I cannot motivate everyone—from the division's chief down to the newest seaman—and inspire them to do their best, an adversarial attitude will quickly take hold. By building a relationship between ATG [Afloat Training Group] and a ship based on trust, we have an open pathway of communication that allows me to make recommendations that are more likely to be heeded and acted upon." The quality of the conversations between Labrenz and his listeners makes a big difference in how effectively the ship functions when it next goes to sea.

Simple Secret #1: Ignite Your Enthusiasm

Labrenz admits that naval operations in general can become monotonous and dull over time. It is up to him as a manager to excite his team by helping them to recognize the vital role they play on the ship. According to Labrenz, "I emphasize the necessity of what we do; I lead by excitement and stir up the status quo on watch. I have two options: One is to be cool, calm, collected, under control, and methodical when dealing with circuit outages or I can leap to my feet and start giving sharp, decisive orders. This is a do-as-I-do approach. There are times for the calm approach. There are also times to raise the blood pressure up a notch or two and be vocal, leading from the front and giving others no choice but to follow." Labrenz has lit a fire in himself well before he even meets his new team. He is passionate and excited about his role. Labrenz sees its direct benefit to the safety of his shipmates and the public they protect. Infusing his young crew with the same energy is part of his role and one that he embraces enthusiastically.

Simple Secret #2: Navigate the Way

Simple Secret #2 calls for crafting a clear, specific, and memorable vision. Labrenz taught me what while IT professionals have a technical understanding of the work to be done, delivering a clear vision will help them become more successful as they advance through their careers, whether they remain in the navy or choose careers in the private sector.

"In a fast-paced environment, the navy places a premium on career progression," says Labrenz. He continues:

> If you cannot advance, your services are not required. Because of this fact of life, an inspiring leader must continually and actively encourage his or her people to study for qualification, advancement exams, certifications, and to continue work toward a college degree. Continuous learning is the key. A "Deck Plate" leader must construct and communicate a vision of achievement. The achievement motive will cause each and every person to take the extra initiative and truly apply themselves to their job. Not everyone wants to stay past their initial enlistment; some are not even content with being in the navy at all. However, a clear and compelling vision will appeal to their aspirations. You may have a future master chief, very career-minded, who will respond well to a prescription for following a set career path. Specific career milestones encourage these people to do their best. You may also have someone whose entire goal is to complete four years

of service and complete their education. For these people, emphasize skills they will be able to use later in the job market. These two people are both responsible for doing the same job. The key is to appeal to both of them in such a way that each will be compelled to do their job exceedingly well.

Labrenz takes a smart approach to communicating with this team. He realizes that two people performing the same job could have very real differences in what they hope to get out of those positions. He helps his crew see a future for themselves based on their career aspirations.

Simple Secret #3: Sell the Benefit

For Labrenz, crafting a clear and compelling vision works hand in hand with Simple Secret #3: selling his team on the benefits of their roles. "A leader must emphasize downstream effects over the specific tasks," says Labrenz. In other words, he succeeds by painting a picture of life for his crew beyond their current assignment. According to Labrenz, "The navy doesn't sell a product or service. We provide a service to the public (i.e., a global maritime environment that is safe and secure for U.S. interests). If you perform well, you will generally advance ahead of your peers and therefore make more money. However, the focus of the message to junior personnel should be on the skills they will learn, the experience to be gained, and even the adventure of a career at sea. This is the internal audience we must motivate aboard ship."

Simple Secret #4: Paint a Picture

"It's interesting that you use the term 'paint a picture,'" I told Labrenz. "I find that inspiring leaders paint verbal pictures by using stories, anecdotes, analogies, metaphors, and other rhetorical devices. How does that apply to your role?"

Labrenz replied:

Nothing is more powerful than a proper sea story at conveying wisdom, experience, and lessons one has learned the hard way. Every good navy leader has an endless supply of sea stories, each with a specific point. This is what separates the effective from the ineffective leader. An effective story may go off target from time to time, but it will always loop back around to the main point and end with a strong lesson. An ineffective story may be entertaining, but it will not impart any worthwhile knowledge. Sea stories are the way we pass down tribal knowledge through the navy. How many corporations have existed since the eighteenth century and still remember their history and traditions?

As you can tell, Labrenz is fiercely loyal to the navy and its obligation to protect U.S. interests and to promote stability. When he forcefully defends the handing down of history and tradition from the eighteenth century, it tells me that stories—and the effective delivery of those stories—is a consistent reminder of a shared vision and values. Tell stories to keep your culture alive and to create fiercely loyal corporate teams who will share the stories and live the lessons those stories impart.

Simple Secret #5: Invite Participation

Simple Secret #5 calls for soliciting feedback, listening to the feedback, and taking action based on what your hear. You wouldn't think that the military would be leading the charge for more openness, but listen to Lorenz address the issue:

The days of one way command-and-control leadership style are over. More and more, the people we recruit want their opinion heard and taken into consideration. A ship at sea is not a democracy, but inclusiveness in decision-making will always deliver better results than forcing an unpopular decision downward through the ranks. If a tough call must be made, sailors will be able to tolerate it if the reasons are made known.

Labrenz says that a ship offers many opportunities for its crew to give feedback, from suggestion boxes to "All Hands" meetings—open forums in every department attended by senior leadership. "How many CEOs of 350,000-employee global enterprises take the time to listen to opinions from the ranks?" he asks.

Informal meetings are also important. Captains often walk around the decks and the mess halls during dinner to learn what's really on the minds of junior personnel. On many Arleigh Burke–class destroyers, the office of the command master chief is adjacent to the mess line. Chatting with the crew over a meal keeps morale high because the crew feel as though they are being heard, and it keeps the ship operating efficiently because senior leaders hear about problems earlier and directly.

Simple Secret #6: Reinforce Optimism

"Pessimism is a cancer that will consume an entire ship," says Labrenz.

Likewise optimism is contagious. Optimism must start from the very top of the structure. If the captain isn't positive, the ship will suffer. Likewise, the wardroom [the officers], the chiefs, on down through senior petty officers to the bottom rung in the ladder, all contribute to overall morale and the climate of the command. An upbeat, can-do, "HOO-YAH" attitude is what differentiates the inspiring leaders from the get-through-the-day task managers.

For optimistic leaders, no obstacle is too big, no setback insurmountable, no request unsupportable. They see the upside of every situation, no matter how dire the conditions have become. Optimism means the difference between life and death for a crew about a navy vessel. The most successful leaders look for the bright side of everything and they communicate the bright vision they see early and often.

Simple Secret #6: Encourage Potential

Spending months at sea would be an arduous task for just about anyone. Imagine what life would be like for those young twenty-something men and women on Labrenz's team if they felt demoralized and apathetic about their roles. Labrenz sees to it that they maintain a culture of cooperation, integrity, and tradition. He is truly concerned for the personal well-being and professional achievement of each and every person who works for him. Where did he learn that quality? From the other great naval leaders before him who communicated their values through the stories they told. A ship's crew must provide its own support network. "When we're at sea, who else can we turn to but each other?" says Labrenz. They can turn to Labrenz because he cares, and they know it.

CHAPTER 9

Fifteen Minutes to Five-Star Service

Fire Starter: Jason Rhodes

Role: Assistant Director of Housekeeping, The Ritz-Carlton, San Francisco

Opportunity: Use an ordinary staff meeting to achieve uncommon results

---

As discussed in Chapter 4, The Ritz-Carlton hotels hold an unusual daily activity intended to inspire and motivate each of its employees worldwide: Each day every department in each hotel around the world holds a "lineup," a fifteen-minute meeting to share information, insights, and stories about employees who went above and beyond expectations to satisfy a hotel guest. After interviewing The Ritz-Carlton president Simon Cooper, I was invited to attend a lineup at the hotel in San Francisco. A stone's throw from the elegant shops at Union Square, The Ritz-Carlton is a monument to neoclassical architecture: The historic

(continued)

building has seventeen massive columns on the outside, making you feel as if you are entering a temple. In a way you are: a temple to sophisticated customer service, unmatched by most hotels in the city.

On one morning at 8:15, I attended a lineup for the hotel's housekeeping staff led by a twenty-six-year-old assistant director named Jason Rhodes. Now, you would expect housekeeping to be a mundane task—replace sheets, vacuum and clean the room. But what surprised me most about this particular group of housekeepers was just how enthusiastic they were about their job. In that meeting—which took place in the basement of the hotel surrounded by rows of laundry machines, sheets, and towels—inspiration took place.

Simple Secret #1: Ignite Their Enthusiasm

When Jason Rhodes accepted the position as the assistant director of housekeeping and laundry of The Ritz-Carlton in San Francisco, he took on the responsibility of inspiring the 110 men and women in the hotel's largest department. It also put him on the fast track to general manager at a Ritz-Carlton hotel. On the morning that I saw him, about fourteen women on the morning shift were assembled for the lineup. They were cheery and enthusiastic, laughing, smiling, and having a good time. They enjoy working at the hotel, and it soon becomes clear why they do.

"Good morning, everyone," Rhodes began with a smile on his face. He was dressed impeccably, in a three-button blue suit, white shirt, purple tie, and shined black shoes. The housekeepers returned an energetic greeting. They connected with Rhodes and were eager to hear from him. Thehousekeepers seemed more excited about their jobs than many people who make five times as much. They like Rhodes and he likes them.

I spoke to Rhodes after the meeting and learned that he stayed in the position longer than is required because he enjoys learning from the mix of employees, including Filipino, Chinese, and African American ethnicities, who reflect the diversity of the city.[1] For managers willing to relocate, especially to Asia, where the chain is booming, The Ritz-Carlton offers incredible opportunities. Rhodes is eager to learn about the cultures and the philosophy of people he will manage as his career progresses, and his enthusiasm rubs off on his staff, creating a sense of teamwork that ultimately leads to five-star customer service.

Simple Secret #2: Navigate the Way

During every lineup, managers take the opportunity to reinforce one of twelve service values that The Ritz-Carlton hotel employees are expected to work by. On this day Rhodes discussed "service value #2," which states "I am always responsive to the expressed and unexpressed wishes and needs of our guests." Rhodes applied this to the housekeepers using examples:

"What is an expressed wish?" Rhodes asked the group.

"If a guest asks for extra pillows," a woman said.

"That's exactly right," he said. "But it's the *unexpressed* wishes that create The Ritz-Carlton mystique," he continued, offering the example of a housekeeper who notices a champagne bottle sitting in melted ice and replaces the ice before being asked to do so.

Simple Secret #3: Sell the Benefit

Rhodes follows up the vision of the day by immediately selling the benefit behind it.

"Why do we do it?" he asks.

"Because we go the extra mile," one housekeeper volunteered.

"We do," says Rhodes. "It offers a personal touch that shows we care. It reflects our commitment to five-star service."

Simple Secret #5: Invite Participation

Rhodes encourages the housekeepers to offer feedback, and they have no trouble giving it. They are encouraged to speak up, and they know Rhodes will listen. He has built a reputation for being willing to listen and for taking immediate action based on the feedback. On this morning the housekeepers were debating the benefit of one cleaner over another. It seemed as though they preferred their old cleaner instead of a new one. A rather mundane discussion, I thought. But I noticed something about Rhodes. He was listening intently, as if this discussion were the most important event in his life at the moment: nodding, making and holding eye contact, and asking questions. He showed genuine and intense interest in the topic. If it is important to his staff, it is important to him.

"Why do you think you have earned so much respect from your staff?" I later asked.

"Because I listen to their concerns," Rhodes said. "And they know I will follow up."

Simple Secret #7: Encourage Their Potential

When Rhodes must instruct someone on how to improve a task, he does so without berating. Focusing on what an employee has done wrong is "demoralizing," he says. Instead, he recognizes the individual's positive contributions as much as possible.

"You did a great job this week cleaning the coffee pot," Rhodes will say, "but you're still struggling here . . . let's work together on improving it." As far as I know, Rhodes is not familiar with the Magic 5:1

Ratio of praise to criticism that Jim Thompson introduced in Chapter 7, but he follows it. Rhodes praises his employees publicly during the lineups and privately as he encourages them to do their best work. By sandwiching the criticism in the middle of praise, he inspires his employees to exceed the expectations of the hotel's guests. When an employee succeeds, he compliments him or her in front of the employee's peers, which serves to gain the admiration of that person's colleagues. By making people feel better about themselves, Rhodes succeeds at the toughest role a manager has: motivating a team to achieve uncommon results.

I chose this example to make a key point: Inspiration can and should take place everywhere within an organization, beyond the chief executive's office. Ritz-Carlton president Simon Cooper cannot personally motivate each of his 35,000 employees worldwide, but with more than 2,700 managers like Rhodes, he doesn't have to. Rhodes reinforces the brand and its values daily for his team. If he can inspire his staff of housekeepers in a fifteen-minute meeting in the laundry room of a hotel, then what's your excuse? Are your employees and colleagues engaged? Are they inspired to follow your vision? Five-star service does not begin with them; it begins with you.

CHAPTER 10

How a Visit to the Lower Ninth Ward Inspired a Nation of Givers

Fire Starter: Peter Fleischer

Role: New Business Pitchman

Opportunity: Create and deliver an exciting new business pitch that captures the hearts and minds of your clients

Peter Fleischer is a partner and new business counselor for Ketchum, a leading global public relations firm. Although he is based in Ketchum's Chicago office, Fleisher is a part-time resident of New Orleans. When the costliest hurricanes ever to hit the United States devastated south Louisiana in August 2005, state leaders created the Louisiana Recovery Authority (LRA) to secure federal dollars. After meeting resistance from some members of Congress, the group decided it would be best to solicit the help of a public relations and public affairs agency. Fleischer led a team that won the account and successfully helped the LRA gain passage of an emergency appropriations bill that provided Louisiana with $4.2 billion for housing and $3.7 billion for levee repairs.

> I spoke to Fleischer at length about how his team inspired the decision-making committee of the LRA and ultimately persuaded Louisiana governor Kathleen Blanco to give the account to Ketchum and its public affairs arm, the Washington Group. For Fleischer, it all began with Simple Secret #1.

Simple Secret #1: Ignite Your Enthusiasm

Fleischer first heard about the pitch on his sabbatical. What he was doing says everything about why he ultimately won the business: In December 2005, Fleischer was in New Orleans aiding the recovery efforts. Hurricanes Katrina and Rita earlier in the year had left parts of Louisiana in ruins. The city of New Orleans, once home to some 450,000 people, became uninhabitable. More than 200,000 homes and 18,000 businesses were destroyed. "This was personal for me," Fleischer says. "We were not going to lose this on my watch. I would do whatever I could to win this."[1]

The hurricanes destroyed parts of New Orleans but not Fleischer's passion for the city and its culture. Rebuilding the city he loved had lit a fire in Fleischer's heart well before the pitch came to his attention. His enthusiasm for the project would ultimately help his team win the account, but he had to make sure the rest of the team shared his deep and personal commitment to the city. Once the team was in place to "rehearse" the pitch, Fleischer decided to bring everyone on a tour of the Lower Ninth Ward to see the devastation for themselves. No facts, no figures, no PowerPoint presentations could replace the direct experience of seeing the shattered remains of a once vibrant city. Fleischer knew it.

After the tour, the entire team shared Fleischer's determination, not only to win the account but to win the business for the good of the city and its people. It showed on their faces and in their voices.

According to Fleischer, "We went into the pitch with emotion, passion and power from having experienced the kind of devastation none of us could ever imagine. It was almost like we still had the dirt on our feet. I got tears in my eyes during the presentation. We did not use PowerPoint slides. We just spoke from the heart. By the time we left the room, the LRA had made the decision to bring our agency to the governor for her final approval." The governor gave Ketchum her blessing before the team had left the room; the pitch was that powerful.

Simple Secret #5: Invite Participation

In addition to lighting a fire in the hearts of his colleagues who would accompany him on the pitch, Fleischer knew he could win the business only if the team brought something new to the table—observations and strategies the LRA had not considered. Fleischer's team went on a listening tour. They invited participation by key stakeholders: members of the Louisiana delegation to Congress, critical legislators, the media, and the general public. Listening to stakeholders is not enough, however, to develop a winning pitch. It's what you do with the information you learn that makes all the difference. According to Fleischer, "If you can't take that information and convert it into something useful, it's a waste of time. In many new business pitches, people will come in and say 'This is what we learned from our research.' Clients will snore their way through it because it is just what the prospect told them. The trick is to arrive to a different conclusion by taking the same information. Every step in the process should add value, not to repeat facts, figures, and research."

By identifying the right people to ask and by listening to their responses, Fleischer and his team determined that a "Katrina fatigue" had set in on the part of the media and general public. They needed a new approach to messaging; a way to remind the public and Congress of just how critical southern Louisiana had become to the U.S. economy and why it was vital to bring it back. By interviewing members of Congress, the team also learned that lawmakers from other states did not believe the Louisiana delegation was sufficiently grateful for what Congress had already done. This reflected a need to show more appreciation to Congress, the media, and the general American public and again to demonstrate why rebuilding Louisiana would be in the entire nation's economic and cultural interests.

Simple Secret #3: Sell the Benefit

Selling the benefit of working with Ketchum was easy. Most large PR agencies bring the top leaders to make a pitch, but after the account is won, the daily work goes to junior professionals. Some are very good. Others need more experience. Bottom line: In far too many cases, the people who make new business pitches are often scarce once they land the business. If you plan to retain a PR agency, especially a large one, always ask who will be the day-to-day contact on the account and demand to meet everyone on the team. Fleischer and his team did not wait for this question. They made it clear that the team in the pitch—with all the passion they brought to the revitalizing the city and the experience they had on Capitol Hill—would be the people directly involved in the program. If the LRA would buy into the integrity of the Ketchum team, their power to get things done, their insight and their passion, the same group making the pitch would be the same individuals working on their behalf.

Simple Secret #4: Paint the Picture

Most new business pitches include a heavy dose of PowerPoint, usually far too many slides, and too many words on each slide. There are times, of course, when a well-structured PowerPoint presentation is expected and required. But inspiring communicators are good storytellers, and good stories use different rhetorical devices, as described in Chapter 4. For the LRA pitch, Fleischer decided to do something he knew the other agencies wouldn't have the guts to: He threw out the slide show and the script. The entire "presentation" was delivered from the heart. Each member of the team got up and, without notes, talked about the impact the devastation had had on them and what it would mean to them personally to help the great city recover. According to Fleischer, "When you throw away the script and speak from the heart with a level of honesty that is rare in business, some pretty remarkable things can happen."

Remarkable things *did* happen. Fleischer's team created a three-pronged strategy to communicate with Capitol Hill and the media, and to thank the American public. The New Orleans spirit was everywhere. On "Fat Tuesday," every congressional office received traditional King Cake and Mardi Gras beads along with a thank-you letter from Governor Blanco. Opinion pieces and letters to the editor were placed on behalf of LRA spokespeople, who made themselves accessible to the media before and after key legislative milestones. When the media converged on New Orleans for the one-year anniversary of Katrina, Fleischer's team managed the messaging, branded the theme of the anniversary as one of rebirth, and conducted extensive media tours to highlight the progress being made with federal dollars.

Fleischer's passion provided the spark that ultimately won the account. The successful pitch provided a win for Fleischer, Ketchum, and the people of Louisiana, who would ultimately receive more than $7 billion from the partnership.

Keep in mind you do not have to experience a tragedy of this magnitude to demonstrate a level of passion and commitment to do the best job you can for your client. But do get personally invested in your clients' business. Get dirt on your feet, as Fleischer did when he visited the Lower Ninth Ward before the pitch. Take the time to ask questions and to really know your prospects' business. It shows that you are listening. If you have a retail client, visit the store as a team, share the experience together. Are you pitching a fast-food client? Enjoy a meal there together. Brainstorm in the environment in which you will be expected to be an expert. Infuse enthusiasm among your entire team, solicit input from key stakeholders, tell a story that is appropriate for the culture, and create a shared experience by visiting the "Lower Ninth Ward." This will help you bring a level of passion to the pitch that will seal the deal.

CHAPTER 11

Wow 'Em Like Steve Jobs

Fire Starter: Steve Jobs
Role: Captivating Pitchman
Opportunity: Inspire employees, customers, and investors in new product presentations

Comparing a Steve Jobs presentation to most presentations is nearly impossible—he's in a league all his own. It would be like comparing a silent movie to *Independence Day*. Where do you start? In my opinion, Apple chief executive Steve Jobs is the most charismatic pitchman in business today. His presentations are brilliant demonstrations of visual storytelling that motivate customers, employees, investors, and the entire computer industry.

The Apple Web site streams his keynotes, which can be used as learning tools. After you read this chapter, visit the Apple site, select "Quicktime" and "Apple Events," and watch a presentation for yourself. You will find that Jobs has mastered all of the 7 Simple Secrets.

In January 2007 Jobs gave perhaps his greatest presentation to introduce the new iPhone.[1] As I expected, the content of his speech met the qualities shared by inspiring leaders. Here are a few ways Jobs wowed the audience.

Simple Secret #1: Ignite Your Enthusiasm

Steve Jobs is passionate about designing cool, fun, and easy-to-use computers, digital music players, and now phones. And he's not too bashful to admit it. His words and phrases reflect his enthusiasm. These quotes are from the iPhone launch and from previous presentations:

> "We're going to make some history together today . . ."
> "Today we're introducing revolutionary products . . ."
> "We've got amazing stuff to show you this morning . . ."
> "This is an awesome computer . . ."
> "This is an incredible way to have fun . . ."
> "This is the coolest thing we've done with video . . ."
> "We are so excited about this. It's incredible . . ."

Many of my clients will acknowledge that Jobs is exciting to hear, and most of them consider him to be a role model for their own presentations. Rarely, however, do these same speakers take the opportunity to express their excitement about a particular product, feature, or service. Most people might be passionate about their story, but when asked to deliver that message in front of others, they fall into presentation mode: serious, glum, stiff, and formal. It's an old speaking style that will leave your listeners uninspired. If you honestly believe that something is "amazing," go ahead and say it. As listeners, we are giving you permission to be excited and passionate and to have fun!

Simple Secret #2: Navigate the Way

Jobs has always been able to craft a vision so vivid and powerful, he rallies his listeners to the better future he sees and, in so doing, persuades them to go along for the ride. In a famous story, Jobs was attempting to lure then Pepsi-CEO John Sculley to lead Apple. Sculley was reluctant. Jobs turned to him and said, "Do you want to sell sugar water all of your life or do you want to change the world?" Jobs's vision is to change the world, and we believe him.

"This is a day I've been looking forward to for two and a half years," Jobs said during the iPhone launch. "Every once in a while, a revolutionary product comes along that changes everything. One would be fortunate to work on just one of these in your career. Apple has been very fortunate to introduce a few of these in the world." At this point in the presentation, Jobs reminds his audience about Apple's previous products that have changed entire industries, like the Macintosh in 1984 and the iPod in 2001. This gives listeners permission to believe in the vision he is about to describe: "Today Apple is going to reinvent the phone!" To reinvent the phone. This mantra, or declaration, is simple, bold, and reflects a concise core purpose that is easy for listeners to remember and to rally around. Note that the one-liner—Today Apple is going to reinvent the phone—is also under ten words.

Simple Secret #3: Sell the Benefit

Once Jobs reveals his one-liner—his core vision—he immediately launches into a discussion of why the world needs a new phone. A solution is inspiring only when it cures a real-world pain. Jobs sells the benefit of the phone by first describing the current state of the industry. The problem, he says, "is they [smart phones like the BlackBerry or Palm Treo] are not that smart and they are not that easy to use. . . . we want to make a leapfrog product that is way smarter than any mobile device has ever been and super easy to use. That is what iPhone is." Jobs continues to describe the problem on most smart phones as being the keyboard—an issue BlackBerry users are familiar with. According to Jobs, keyboards represent a problem because they take up more than one-third of the phone and are permanent, whether the person is using them or not. The Apple solution is to create a "revolutionary interface" that will get rid of the buttons and create one giant screen. This brings up the problem—how do you get around the screen with no scroll wheel or stylus? Again, Jobs sets up a problem and offers a solution: "We're going to use the best pointing device in the world," he says. "A device we're all born with. Our fingers." Jobs then describes Apple's new "multi-touch" technology that accurately responds to the touch of a finger to bring up applications on the phone.

To recap, Jobs sells the benefits of the iPhone in three steps:

1. Review the state of the industry.
2. Describe limitations of existing products.
3. Explain how Apple has found solutions for these problems.

Where most speakers describe the solution before the problem, Jobs flips it around. It makes the story more interesting and easier for the listener to follow.

Simple Secret #4: Paint a Picture

Jobs tells the iPhone story by using several techniques:

1. *Stick to the rule of three.* We remember lists in groups of three. Jobs unveils the iPhone and builds drama at the same time by saying, "Today we are introducing *three* revolutionary products

[an image of each product appears on the screen as he mentions each one]. "The first is a wide-screen iPod with touch controls, the second is a revolutionary mobile phone, and the third is a breakthrough Internet communications device." For added emphasis and drama, he repeats the three products and he repeats them three times: "An iPod, a phone, an Internet communicator.... Are you getting it?" Jobs says. He then delivers the knockout: "These are not three separate devices. This is one device! Today Apple is going to reinvent the phone!" The dramatic buildup takes several minutes and is met with enthusiastic cheers. It is incredible to watch. Jobs conducts a presentation like a symphony, with ebbs and flows, buildups and climaxes. It leaves his listeners wildly excited.

2. *Tell personal stories.* During one section of the presentation, Jobs's clicker to advance the slides suddenly stops working. He mentions it with a smile, knowing that somebody backstage will take care of it. Jobs kills time by telling a personal story about how he and Apple cofounder Steve Wozniak had built a TV jammer and used it to block TV signals at Wozniak's college dorm. Jobs had turned a minor glitch into an opportunity to make an emotional connection with his audience. Personal stories or anecdotes show us his human side. The audience laughed, smiled, and was kept amused as technicians repaired the glitch. Jobs continues as if it had all been planned. Effortless but powerful.

3. *Keep it visual.* In a Steve Jobs presentation, you will not find bullet points on any slide; not one. You will not see slides filled with mind-numbing data, numbers, or words. The slides are highly visual. A photograph or image is all he needs. When Jobs outlined the three products—an iPod, a phone, an Internet communicator—a slide with an image of each product appeared

as he mentioned each one: one slide, one product (an iPod, a phone, and a computer). It struck a perfect balance between the visual and the verbal. The simplicity of the slides kept the audience focused on the speaker: Steve Jobs. When he discussed the "ultimate pointing device"—your fingers—all the audience saw on the screen behind Jobs was an image of the iPhone and a finger touching it. Every slide was big on images and low on text. Images are memorable and, more important, complement the speaker, where the audience attention should be focused. Too much text on a slide distracts from the speaker's words. Strike the right balance between visual and verbal.

4. *Rehearse.* I know as a fact from speaking to people at Apple that Jobs rehearses presentations for hours. Nothing is taken for granted. He knows the flow of his story, how he is going to build up to a big moment, what he is going to demonstrate, and how he will open and close the presentation. He appears effortless but only after hours of rehearsal. Motivation takes preparation.

Simple Secret #6: Reinforce an Optimistic Outlook

Nobody launches revolutionary products without an optimistic outlook. Since his earliest days of tinkering with computers, Jobs has had an unshakable belief that his products would change the world. In each of his presentations, Jobs speaks the language of hope and opportunity. Near the end of his iPhone launch, Jobs said, "There's an old Wayne Gretzky quote that I love. 'I skate to where the puck is going to be, not where it has been.' We've always tried to do that at Apple since the very beginning and we always will." Always end your presentations on a hopeful note.

Simple Secret #7: Encourage Others to Reach Their Potential

Jobs asked a team to work around the clock for two years to create the iPhone. Participating in the creation of a revolutionary product certainly must have kept them energized. But Jobs capped off their effort by asking them to stand, publicly praising them at the end of his presentation. He recognizes the team behind his success and acknowledges them to others. How do you think his employees would have felt if Jobs had taken all the credit? It would have been demoralizing. Instead, they were praised in front of their families and thousands of media, analysts, peers, and partners who were assembled for the launch.

You owe it to yourself to watch a Jobs presentation on the Apple Web site. Jobs does not use a presentation merely to convey information. A Jobs presentation excites, inspires, and motivates and, in doing so, turns customers into evangelists.

CHAPTER 12

How an Ice Cream Shop Became the Hottest Franchise in Town

Fire Starter: Doug Ducey
Role: Selling a vision for the ultimate ice cream experience
Opportunity: Persuading current and potential franchisees to buy into a business with a goal toward becoming the best-selling ice cream brand in America

---

If you love ice cream, you owe it to yourself to visit a Cold Stone Creamery. When you do, do not plan on counting calories. You will find dozens of rich, creamy, delectable flavors. Pick your ice cream and your toppings, and watch as young clerks scoop the ice cream onto cold granite slabs and mix in the ingredients. It's like the Benihana of ice cream. If you have trouble deciding on a combination, it's no problem. They have gut-busting suggestions, such as the Founder's Favorite: sweet ice cream, pecans, brownie, fudge, and caramel.

Cold Stone is also known for entertainment. Place a tip in the jar and watch as the employees sing a song. Corny? Not really.

(continued)

Adults and kids love the combination and have kept the chain growing at a stunning pace. Today there are more than 1,400 Cold Stone stores around the United States. It is the third largest ice cream shop chain and the fourteenth largest franchise. Cold Stone chief executive Doug Ducey captures all of the 7 Simple Secrets in his professional communications, but a few in particular helped him turn Cold Stone into one of the hottest brands in America.[1]

Simple Secret #2: Navigate the Way

I never realized the world of ice cream could be so competitive. But it is. Not that I'm complaining. Much to my delight, there are plenty of ice cream shops to choose from: Dairy Queen, BaskinRobbins, TCBY, and others. These choices have created intense competition in the industry known as "scoop shop" chains. In the face of these entrenched brands, Cold Stone Creamery CEO Doug Ducey unveiled a bold vision in 1999: "The world will know us as the 'Ultimate Ice Cream Experience' by making us the number-one best-selling ice cream brand in America by December 31, 2009!" To appreciate just how wild this sounded at the time, you have to understand that there were only seventy-four Cold Stone franchise shops operating when Ducey made his announcement. Dairy Queen alone had well over 5,000. Was this vision just the heady goal of a leader who had enjoyed one too many servings of chocolate-chip cookie dough? Not at all. Ducey knew exactly what he was doing, and he understood the power of a well-crafted vision expertly delivered.

Ducey thought about the vision statement carefully before announcing it publicly. "Experience" had to be included to differentiate Cold Stone from the other ice cream shops. He knew that fans of Cold Stone had an emotional connection to the brand. Of course the ice cream—made fresh daily—played a part in establishing this devotion.

But the emotional engagement came from what Ducey dubbed "The X-Factor": the mix of entertainment and energy that has turned Cold Stone from just another ice cream shop to a destination where lines often can be out the door. Children and adults line up to watch energetic teenagers sing, dance, banter, mix, and serve Cold Stone's decadent ice cream creations. Instead of interviews, the chain actually holds "auditions" to find the best teens to work at its stores. (Ducey tells me the Times Square location in New York is quite a sight. One teen who worked there landed a role in the Broadway version of *Grease*!) Since the experience had everything to do with the emotional attachment ice cream lovers had with the brand, the experience had to be the core of the vision.

Ducey understands the minds of franchise owners: entrepreneurs who can sniff out bull a mile away. His vision had to be big and bold but also believable and achievable. The vision had to have specific, measurable, and attainable goals attached to it. After asking for feedback and carefully reviewing the company's growth with current franchise owners and executives (Simple Secret #5: Invite Participation), Ducey made the vision tangible by setting a specific number of new store openings by a specific date: one thousand stores by December 31, 2004. The plan was ambitious by anyone's standards, but Ducey had the hard numbers to back it up including the fact that Cold Stone franchises were boasting the highest average sales-per-unit in the ice cream industry. According to Ducey, "It was a grand vision that would require hard work—it would get us up early, keep us up late, and tap all our energies and skills." It was a stretch goal but achievable, believable, and consistent with the company's core values. Once Ducey announced it publicly, it set momentum in motion. Over the next five years, the vision took on a life of its own, inspiring the entire Cold Stone team of employees and franchise owners to make it come true. But crafting and articulating the vision were just the beginning to getting ultimate buy-in. Ducey had to sell the benefit behind it.

Simple Secret #3: Sell the Benefit

Franchise owners are a tough group of folks who have no qualms about asking the hard questions. They take pleasure at throwing verbal hatchets at CEOs. A leader of a franchise chain had better be able to catch and deflect those hatchets if he hopes to survive. For franchisees, a vision statement means nothing unless it has something in it for them. Ducey knew that after delivering a bold vision for growth, each and every one of the franchise owners would be asking themselves, "What's in it for me?" Ducey was prepared to communicate five "brand benefits" behind the vision: higher sales, lower costs, higher profits, more marketing dollars, and higher asset values.

As Ducey explained to the franchise owners, brands that grow from the local, to the regional, to the national enjoy higher sales than their competitors. A rising ice cream tide would raise everyone's boat. Size would also provide leverage with vendors to lower material and ingredient costs. Higher sales and lower costs would make them more profitable, and of course a profitable business would be necessary to sustain continued success as a brand. Ducey also taught franchise owners the lessons he had learned about bigger brands attracting more marketing dollars. "If I have one store and put Oreos in my cookies and cream ice cream, Nabisco won't even know I exist. Give me a couple of hundred stores and the Nabisco's brand manager will fly on a plane to visit me," he would tell his audience. And finally, Ducey appealed to the franchise owners' passion: investment and growth. They would be purchasing an asset that will be worth more tomorrow than it is today.

In all of his communications, Ducey puts himself in the shoes of a franchise owner. He makes sure the benefit is clear by asking himself; "If I were a franchise owner, what's in it for me?" For example, something as simple as a new menu board might not sound like such a big deal, but if headquarters is asking franchise owners to spend $300 on it, the plan will be met with some skepticism. According to Ducey, the key to motivating franchise owners in that case would be to tie in the proposal to one of the five brand benefits outlined earlier. In the case of a new menu board, Ducey would explain that the investment will result in higher sales by educating consumers about the variety of items available, including shakes, smoothies, cakes, and ice cream flavors. Your listeners are constantly asking "What's in it for me?" Any attempt at motivation will fall short if you fail to answer that key question.

Simple Secret #4: Paint a Picture

Ducey had announced an energizing vision and inspired his stakeholders to buy into the vision by selling the benefit behind the goal. But what I find even more fascinating from a leadership communications perspective is how Ducey handled the deadline event. Remember, he had set December 31, 2004, as the deadline for reaching the goal of 1,000 stores. Franchise owners gathered at the annual conference in January 2005 for an update. Just one problem—Cold Stone had missed its goal by about 100 stores. Ducey took careful pains to craft the story for maximum impact. He stood up and, borrowing a line from football legend Vince Lombardi, said that Lombardi never lost a game, he just ran out of time.

They had not failed, he said. He reminded franchise owners to look at the vision statement carefully. The vision statement had been accompanied by a set of core values, one of which was to "Do the right thing." He told a personal story about the day the vice president of franchising and real estate stepped into his office to tell him they could hit the goal *if* they cut corners on franchisee selection and locations. The answer was obvious to everyone: The core value of "Do the right thing" had to take precedence over a self-imposed goal outlined several years earlier. Ducey told the franchise owners assembled at the conference that everyone would benefit by having the right people in the right places. Every one should be proud of every single franchise in the system. He reminded them that the "vision"—to create the ultimate ice cream experience—was still alive. One thousand stores would be a result of achieving that vision, but being true to their values would be more important over the long run. Ducey told them he was confident they would hit the goal by April, given the number of applications in the system. Indeed, Cold Stone hit its goal just four months past a deadline that had been imposed five years earlier.

By putting the vision in perspective through the stories he told and by remaining optimistic (Simple Secret #6), Ducey left his franchise owners even *more* inspired than if he had actually hit the goal!

Simple Secret #7: Encourage Their Potential

Cold Stone faces the same challenge many retail and restaurant chains confront: encouraging young teenagers to provide outstanding customer service when they'd rather be uploading videos to YouTube. Ducey acknowledges that Cold Stone positions are entry level. A sixteen-year-old does not dream of having the same job scooping ice cream when she turns twenty-six. The Cold Stone approach is to inspire teenagers by encouraging them to use the position to learn life skills that will serve them well later in life, whether they become CEOs or stay-at-home moms. Franchise owners and managers are encouraged to reinforce to teenagers that Cold Stone is "the best first job" they could ever have. Teenagers are told they will learn life skills that will help them become more successful in interviews, jobs, and careers: communicating with peers and customers, team building, decision making, accountability, and how a vision manifests itself in day-to-day operations. Singing and talking to customers also helps shy or awkward teenagers come out of their shells. According to Ducey, learning to work in a retail environment where customers want to return again and again teaches teens valuable skills they can put to use in any career they choose.

Simple Secret #1: Ignite Your Enthusiasm

A franchise like Cold Stone cannot succeed without the energetic commitment of its founders, CEO, franchisees, managers, and employees. At the end of the day, they're selling ice cream. You either love the business or you don't. According to Ducey, it is not a restaurant, it is an ice cream store, which means you have to deal with teenagers and you make money in small increments of $2 waffle cones. It is not for everyone. But those who are passionate about it can infuse that enthusiasm throughout their store. Cold Stone attracts people who are passionate about making other people happy. Ice cream just provides the means to do it.

CHAPTER 13

A Mission Impossible Fit for Tom Cruise

Fire Starter: Matt McCauley

Role: Chief executive officer of a children's clothing giant

Opportunity: Jump-start a major retailer by rallying employees, partners, and vendors around a mission most people considered impossible

Chances are you can find a Gymboree store at your local mall. With more than 600 retail stores across America, the colorful Gymboree clothing stores have become must-visit destinations for moms looking to outfit their children in the colorful, cute and trendy clothes. Okay, I'll admit dropping in myself now and then to find something for my baby daughters. Before kids, I never thought about the perfect Easter dress or the latest fall fashions for babies and children. I sure do now!

Matt McCauley is the young, charismatic chief executive of the chain. According to *Forbes* magazine, McCauley was one of the youngest CEOs of a publicly traded company when he took the reins at the age of thirty-two. I've met McCauley a few times and had the opportunity to interview him here. McCauley sparked a change in philosophy that reenergized the brand; driving up the company's growth, profits, and stock price.[1] McCauley brings new energy to the chain, which he admits was struggling for direction in 2004 before he took over. In February 2007 McCauley sat down with me to discuss his approach for motivating people to break through barriers. You will see that McCauley's techniques reinforce the 7 Simple Secrets model and apply equally to CEOs, managers, entrepreneurs, and anyone else who needs to inspire a team.

Simple Secret #1: Ignite Your Enthusiasm

McCauley is inspired by accomplishing things people say cannot be done. Tell Matt McCauley that something cannot be done and you've fired him up. "When I think about inspiring leaders, every one was obsessed with making a difference, to change something, to do something different," McCauley tells me. McCauley genuinely wants to make a difference in the lives of his employees and customers. He is "obsessed" with progress in his professional and personal life—to be a better leader, husband, and father. He had worked at Gymboree for five years prior to being named chief executive officer. When he saw the opportunity to reinvigorate the brand, he jumped in and announced some very ambitious goals—some would say "absurd" goals—because he was excited about what the brand could become and how it would improve the lives of all of Gymboree's employees and customers. McCauley's passion, energy, and enthusiasm sent Gymboree into orbit.

Simple Secret #2: Navigate the Way

Nobody will ever accuse McCauley of failing to dream big—really big. In 2005, after what had been a difficult year of transition, McCauley announced to the Gymboree board that he believed the company could double its earnings in a couple of years. He was wrong. Gymboree did it in one year. His vision set in motion the collective creativity of thousands of people who worked for Gymboree and its partners.

Some people thought the goal was absurd. Others laughed out loud. That was the point. McCauley intentionally set a goal he calls "mission impossible," a goal that most people say cannot be accomplished. According to McCauley:

> Every team, every department, every individual should have goals that are impossible to reach. A lot of people would say that it could be discouraging. I feel quite the opposite. I think setting impossible goals is the only way one can find out what you are truly capable of. Here's what happens: Instead of finding obstacles, the conversation changes. People start saying "Well, we know it probably can't happen but it might if we change this, or do this differently or change our approach in this area," then the mission impossible forces people to think differently, feel differently and behave differently. That's what impossible goals do!

Amazing, isn't it? McCauley has discovered that setting outrageous goals stimulates ideas that had never been considered. The result speaks for itself—the company met McCauley's goal one year ahead of the goal he had set himself!

McCauley adds one important caveat to this approach. "Mission impossibles" can result in frustration if your team does not "celebrate like crazy" when they hit key milestones. Big, crazy dreams can be incredibly exciting, but people must believe progress is being made. When they see that progress and celebrate accomplishments, the big vision begins to feel real. Obstacles seem small in comparison.

Simple Secret #3: Sell the Benefit

McCauley could not propose a plan to double earnings and leave it at that. He had to sell the benefit behind accomplishing that goal. He had to put himself in the shoes of the individuals he was attempting to persuade. "Why should they care?" he would ask himself. McCauley would visit factories around the world to persuade them to give Gymboree better prices. He would meet with factory owners face to face to learn what was important to them. Some asked for larger orders while others desired more stability or consistency of orders. Once he understood where the factory owners were coming from, he could craft a persuasive response. "If bigger orders are important to you," McCauley would say, "then here's why you will benefit from giving us better prices. If you give us better prices, 100 percent of those savings will be reinvested in opening new stores and in marketing. That means higher sales and a larger inventory for us and bigger orders for you."

"Matt, when you proposed the vision to double your company's earnings, how did you sell the benefit of your vision to employees who might not be concerned about stock price?" I asked.

"For some of our employees, especially moms with kids, flexible work hours are important while others look for more money or career growth. Help people understand how the vision will help them get what they want." For working mothers, a rising stock would mean a more prosperous company, which would allow Gymboree to offer a better package of benefits including flexible schedules. For those who want more money, a rising stock would lead to larger bonuses. McCauley cannot inspire without answering the question "What's in it for me?" So he always does.

Simple Secret #5: Invite Participation

Painting a vision of what you plan to accomplish is meaningless unless everyone who plays a part in reaching the goal feels as if he or she plays an important role in making it come true. According to McCauley, "Every function, every division, every person, needs their own 'mission impossible' that all adds up to the ultimate vision." McCauley did not just announce the goal of doubling revenue; he said: "Let's set the

impossible goal together." Gymboree is made up of dozens of departments: real estate, production, merchandising, design, finance, and so
on. Every group, every member of the team, was encouraged to find
new ways to drive revenue or trim expenses. Once every member of a
group saw how he or she participated in the vision and was asked for input, their collective talent to make the dream come true was unleashed.

Simple Secret #6: Reinforce an Optimistic Outlook

The entire concept of a mission impossible reflects McCauley's optimistic view of the world. It took optimism for a thirty-two-year-old to
walk into a board meeting of a publicly trade company and outline
a goal most people would think impossible to reach. McCauley has
discovered that setting a mission impossible and selling the benefit
behind the vision would get people excited to reach the goal together.
The more excited people get, the less time they spend on making ex-
cuses for why it can't happen and the more mental effort they expend
on figuring out how to make it come true.

Simple Secret #7: Encourage Others to Reach Their Potential

Setting a mission impossible actually fostered creativity and allowed
employees to bring out the potential of the company. "The biggest
change was clarity," says McCauley. "There is comfort and security in
clarity. People become anxious when they do not see where they are
going. They need to see the plan and feel as though they are a part of it.
They need to recognize exactly what they did to contribute to the company's success. Vision and clarity brings security." What happens when
you feel secure? You can take risks. You stop acting out of fear. Fear
stifles creativity because you are afraid to make mistakes. McCauley

encouraged his employees to reach their potential by providing clarity and removing the fear factor.

At the time of this writing, McCauley has led a massive turnaround at Gymboree, stunning analysts, gratifying investors, and giving employees a new purpose, vision, and confidence in the future. Is McCauley's success all due to his ability to inspire his listeners? Of course not. But it's a big part of it. I asked a leading CEO recruiter what was more important: operational knowledge or the ability to inspire. "The ability to inspire is huge," she said. "A leader might be operationally brilliant but will never make the most of his ability without inspiring the people around him." McCauley's extensive retail and merchandising experience was a plus, but it was not enough to propel his team to greatness. Accomplishing the mission impossible required a team absolutely committed to their leader and his vision. McCauley's ability to set a vision and to rally people around it made the difference.

CHAPTER 14

A Master Class in Motivation

Fire Starter:	Ron Clark
Role:	Teacher of the Year
Opportunity:	Encourage a group of underachieving students to exceed the expectations of their peers, parents, teachers, society, and even themselves

I'm a sucker for an underdog story. I must have watched *Rocky* a half dozen times in the theater when it first came out. I can't tell you how many times I've watched *Hoosiers, Seabiscuit, 8 Mile, Braveheart, The Pursuit of Happyness,* and *Remember the Titans.* If it's a story of overcoming seemingly insurmountable odds, I'm there. So it came as no surprise that a made-for-TV movie caught my attention: the *Ron Clark Story* on TNT. *Friends* star Matthew Perry played a teacher who was named Disney's Teacher of the Year in 2000 for taking a class of underperforming fifth graders in Spanish Harlem and turning them around in one school year. By the end of the year, the same fifth graders who had been performing at the second-grade level before Clark entered their lives had outscored even the "gifted" class. In the month the movie aired (August 2006), I read a first-person account from one of Clark's Harlem students. She was a senior in high school at the time and credited Clark with completing her transformation from troublemaker to contributor. Sensing an opportunity to learn something about inspiration, I wanted to talk to Ron Clark myself. He didn't let me down. But first some background.[1]

Clark was teaching the fifth grade in North Carolina when he saw a program about a school in Harlem that had a hard time attracting qualified teachers. He decided to pack his bags and teach there. He traveled to New York, stayed at a YMCA, and ventured out to find a school. He landed at PS 83 in Spanish Harlem. Clark told me there were five levels of fifth grade classes at the school: two classes where students were performing at grade level, two "gifted" classes, and one class performing at the second-grade level in reading and math. Guess which class Clark chose to teach? You got it, the underachievers. The kids in Clark's first class thought this guy from North Carolina had lost his marbles, but they soon began to believe the vision he had set for them. Clark had successfully changed their belief systems—the ultimate goal of inspiration!

By the end of the year, the previously underperforming fifth graders had, indeed, outscored the gifted classes. Clark went on to win Disney's Teacher of the Year award in 2000, appear on *Oprah* several times, write a best-selling book, *The Essential 55,* and build the Ron Clark Academy in Atlanta, which serves students in the fifth to eighth grades from low-income areas. Clark still keeps in touch with students from his Harlem class and is proud to boast that each of the thirty-seven students from his 1999 class was a senior in high school at the time of our interview—not one had dropped out! Clark's lessons apply to teachers, managers, and leaders in any field.

Simple Secret #1: Ignite Your Enthusiasm

After college, Ron Clark had no plans to be a teacher. Instead he embarked on some wild adventures in Europe, finally returning home to North Carolina for a short time. His mother told him about an opening at a local school and convinced him to visit the school. Clark went reluctantly, thinking he would placate his mother and then hit the road again. During a tour of the school, Clark had no interest in teaching until the door opened to the fifth-grade class. A boy looked up and asked if Clark was going to be their new teacher. It was an "epiphany," according to Clark. He spent the next five years teaching there, then left for New York because it was a "calling." Helping students excel is almost a spiritual experience for Clark. There is nothing else he would rather do. When your message becomes a "calling," you know that there is a fire in your heart that is sure to ignite a spark in the people you are trying to reach.

Simple Secret #2: Navigate the Way

Clark's enthusiasm helped him connect with his Harlem class from the day he stepped through the door, but inspiration took hold when he crafted a vision for what they could accomplish: perform at grade level by the end of the school year. Given the fact that the fifth-graders were performing at the second-grade level, this itself represented a "big, hairy, audacious goal" as Jim Collins and Jerry Porras would call it. Nobody was expecting the class to beat the gifted students, but that's the magic of vision—once you start thinking BIG, the world beats a path to you door and your accomplishments can be truly heroic.

Simple Secret #3: Sell the Benefit

"It's not enough to set a goal," Clark told me. You need to tell your people *why* it's important to reach that goal. "For my students, it meant a better future. I told them why they needed to know a certain subject, how it would be an advantage to them in their lives. I would tell them that no matter what they wanted to do in life—whether their goal was to become a professional basketball player or a lawyer—they had to understand money and math or people would take advantage of them. I would show them how learning history would help them live a better life, be a better person and to ultimately be more successful." When it comes to inspiring your listeners, the "why" is often more important than the "how."

Simple Secret #4: Paint a Picture

Clark likes to tell stories to his students. Stories, especially personal ones, help make the lessons real. According to Clark:

> When I was an education student, they told us that we had to set a boundary between teachers and students; that we should not bring up stories from our own life. Bull. Everyday, I tell stories that bring the lessons to life. It's a powerful way to teach. As a leader, talk about the mistakes you have made. It's an endearing quality to say, 'I have made this mistake before and I want to make sure none of you make the same one.' For example, I tell the story about never having met my grandfather even though I wanted to. When I was twenty-three years old, I built up the courage to do it. I called his sister on a Saturday to tell her that I was going to my grandfather's house on Monday. He had a heart attack that Sunday and I never met him. But for years I had been building up the courage to talk to him. I tell that story to

my kids to make the point—don't put things off. If you want to do something, go for it. Don't put it off another day. Make today your today. My students can relate to my story.

Personal stories are motivational because your audience can interpret their current situation through the lens of your experience. Personal stories work in the classroom or in the corporate environment. Tell more of them.

Simple Secret #5: Invite Participation

Clark's students began to care as they learned just how much their new teacher cared about them. Clark said that in 1999, when he began teaching in Harlem, jump-roping was big. Instead of spending lunch in the teacher cafeteria, Clark could be found trying to Double-Dutch in the schoolyard. One of the biggest lessons he learned about being a super-motivator is to show people how much you care about their personal lives and their success. In an article one of his students wrote seven years after Clark first taught her class in Harlem, Tamara Lauriano said that the students began to respect Clark when he showed he cared. "He asked us what was going on in our lives," she wrote.[2] This was a big deal to her and the other students. By showing that he cared about what the students were going through personally, Clark set up the students for success in every aspect of their lives.

Simple Secret #6: Reinforce an Optimistic Outlook

Clark's can-do spirit is infectious. His words reflect his optimism, and he refuses to let any of his students speak the language of defeat.

Rule 50 in Clark's *The Essential 55* states: "Be positive and enjoy life. Some things just aren't worth getting upset over. Keep everything in perspective and focus on the good in your life."[3] Clark told me that a leader must set the tone, especially in the words he chooses to use. It is up to the leader to set high expectations, to praise people, to believe in them, and to do whatever it takes to help people meet their goals, he believes. Despite the significant challenges Clark faced as a teacher, he remained optimistic and steadfast in his belief that the rules would unlock the students' potential.

Simple Secret #7: Encourage Others to Reach Their Potential

Clark's entire story is one of encouragement. But during our conversation, I realized that part of his success had to do with the fact that he got the entire class to celebrate their success as a team. According to Clark:

> All across America, a student is trying to please a teacher. In every corporation, you have individuals trying to please one person, their boss. If you have that type of environment, you can hang it up. Forget it. If you are trying to please one person, your level of success will be minimal. We have to create an environment where everyone wants to lift each other up. If you want a team to be successful, you have to create an atmosphere where everyone is cheering, clapping and patting each other on the back, an atmosphere where everyone on the team is proud of each other. If you set a goal and everyone is working toward that goal as an individual and not as a team, it can be intimidating. But if you feel like you have the support of an entire team—friends, colleagues, coworkers—then you can set the goal as high as you want because there is no fear associated with it. Every person on that team will want to contribute to achieving that goal because they are doing it together.

Clark's Rule 55 sums up his own approach to teaching as well as the principles outlined in this book: Be the best person you can be. "Make sure you are always developing into the kind of person you want to be, and the kind of person others want to be around," writes Clark.[4] This is a great quote to keep in mind as you develop your skills of motivation. By inspiring your listeners, you become the kind of person people want to be around. Companies will want to hire you, customers will want to do business with you, employees will want to work for you, colleagues will want to be on your team, investors will want to back you, and your friends and family will cherish you.

CONCLUSION

Be a Spellbinder

I hope the individuals featured in this book have inspired you as much as they have inspired me. We need more people like them inside and outside of the corporate world.

Not a day goes by when I'm not reminded of the need for more inspiring individuals in our lives. One of my wife's best friends—we'll call her "Rhonda"—had recently dropped in. I overheard the two women discussing Rhonda's resume, which she had just updated. Rhonda is a top salesperson for her company. Nothing wrong with keeping your resume fresh, I thought, but it was a bit odd.

"Rhonda, you're making over six figures, you've only been at the job a year, you're the second-highest-grossing salesperson in the entire company, and you just enjoyed an expenses-paid trip with your husband to Hawaii because you made the President's Club. Why are you looking for a new job?" I asked.

"Carmine, in my case, making the President's Club was a major accomplishment," she said. "I was the first woman to make it in the company's eighteen-year history, and the only thing I expected from my boss was for him to acknowledge it publicly. He never did."

211

Rhonda's boss had failed Simple Secret #7 by not praising Rhonda in front of her peers. She was demoralized despite receiving an expensive trip to Hawaii. By the time you read this, Rhonda will probably be at another job, and her current company will have lost a top salesperson.

I wish I could drill this fact into the heads of leaders in corporate America: Inspiring people is not that complicated. It's rather simple, really. But it does require that you examine how you communicate to the people you intend to motivate. Here's the good news: Developing these skills will help you stand out. In *Rich Dad, Poor Dad*, Robert T. Kiyosaki writes, "It is the ability to sell—therefore, to communicate to another human being, be it a customer, employee, boss, spouse or child—that is the base skill of personal success."[1] Success begins and ends with your ability to communicate an inspiring story.

In an episode from season 6 of *The Apprentice* on NBC, Donald Trump "fired" a contestant who had won more challenges than the others. But the wannabe apprentice lacked the ability to inspire. Before letting the young man go, Trump said, "You have a good record but your team has never been spellbound by you."[2] People are searching for spellbinders at home and in the office. A few of these spellbinders have shared their techniques with us, but there are many others like them. Seek them out. Better yet, be one of them.

When I was writing this book, a song by Natasha Bedingfield was popular; the lyrics go like this: "Live your life with arms wide open. Today is where your book begins. The rest is still unwritten."[3] This is where my book ends and yours begins. I know these techniques will help you sell yourself and your ideas more effectively; but I hope you use your powers of persuasion to inspire others to reach a new level of growth in their personal and professional lives. Use your voice to help others find theirs.

Notes

Part I   Introduction

1. Andrea Strauss as told to Christopher Elliott, "Event Planning, Doing-the-Impossible Division," *New York Times*, December 26, 2006.

2. Andrew Razeghi, *Hope: How Triumphant Leaders Create the Future* (San Francisco: Jossey-Bass, 2006), 28.

3. The Conference Board, "U.S. Job Satisfaction Keeps Falling, The Conference Board Reports Today," February 28, 2005, www .conference-board.org/utilities/pressPrinterFriendly.cfm?press_ID= 2582 (accessed December 19, 2001).

4. Scott L. Kimball and Carl E. Nink, "How to Improve Employee Motivation, Commitment, Productivity, Well-Being and Safety," *Corrections Today* 68, no. 3 (June 1, 2006).

5. Watson Wyatt Worldwide, "Effective Communication: A Leading Indicator of Financial Performance," Communication ROI Study, 2005–2006, www.watsonwyatt.com/research/resrender.asp?id=w-868 &page=1 (accessed March 2, 2007).

6. Jay Conger, "Inspiring Others: The language of leadership," *Academy of Management Executive* 5, no. 1 (1991): 31–45.

Chapter 1   Ignite Your Enthusiasm

1. Marissa Mayer, Vice President, Search Products & User Experience, Google, in discussion with the author, September 21, 2006.

2. Richard Tait, cofounder and CEO, a.k.a. Grand Poo Bah, Cranium, in discussion with the author, November 10, 2006.

3. Krista Hawkins, Specialist-Public Relations Department, Hyundai Motor Manufacturing Alabama, LLC, in discussion with the author, November 8, 2006.

4. Vince Lombardi Jr., *What It Takes to Be #1* (New York: McGraw-Hill, 2001), 103.

5. Jack Welch and Suzy Welch, "How Healthy Is Your Company?" *BusinessWeek*, May 8, 2006.

6. From *Larry King Live*, first aired on October 9, 2006, property of CNN.

7. Tiziana Casciaro and Miguel Sousa Lobo, "Competent Jerks, Lovable Fools, and the Formation of Social Networks," *Harvard Business Review* 83, no. 6 (June 2005): 92–99.

8. Steven R. Covey, "Four Traits of Great Leaders," *Leadership Excellence*, Copyright 1984–2005, Executive Excellence Publishing, www.eep2.com/images/chalk/1105/le021105.htm (accessed March 2, 2007).

9. "The Best Advice I Ever Got: Warren Buffet, Richard Branson, Meg Whitman, A.G. Lafley, and 24 Other Luminaries on the People Who Most Influenced Their Business Lives," *Fortune*, March 21, 2005.

Chapter 2   Navigate the Way

1. Marcus Buckingham, *The One Thing You Need to Know* (New York: Free Press, 2005), 59.

2. Ibid., 61–62.

3. Jack Welch and Suzy Welch, "Don't Play the Office Cop," *BusinessWeek*, December 4, 2006.

4. John A. Byrne, "The Fast Company Interview: Jeff Immelt," *Fast Company*, July 2005.

5. Dilbert Cartoon, February 8, 2005, Copyright 2005 Scott Adams, Distributed by UFS, Inc.

6. Mission Statement Generator function at www.dilbert.com, www.dilbert.com/comics/dilbert/games/career/bin/ms.cgi (accessed March 11, 2007).

7. Doug Ducey, (CEO and Chairman, Cold Stone Creamery, in discussion with the author, January 25, 2007.

8. Wayne Leonard, (Chairman and CEO, Entergy Corporation, in discussion with the author, April 6, 2006.

9. Wayne Leonard, email sent to author, April 2006.

10. Jim Collins and Jerry Porras, *Built to Last, Successful Habits of Visionary Companies* (New York: Collins Business Essentials, 1994), 48.

11. Carleen Hawn, Susanna Hammer, and Erick Schonfeld, "How to Succeed in 2007," *Business* 2.0, December 1, 2006.

12. From *The Big Idea with Donnie Deutsch*, first aired on October 6, 2006, property of CNBC.

13. Collins and Porras, *Built to Last*, 234.

14. Mike McCue, CEO and Cofounder Tellme, in discussion with the author, December 12, 2006.

15. Ryan Blitstein, "Microsoft's Ballmer Gives Business Lessons," *San Jose Mercury News*, March 16, 2007.

16. Richard Tait, Cofounder and CEO, a.k.a. Grand Poo Bah, Cranium, in discussion with the author, November 10, 2006.

17. Steve Hamm and William C. Symonds, "Mistakes Made on the Road to Innovation; Led by CEO Antonio M. Perez, Kodak is struggling to reinvent its business model. It's Not Alone," *BusinessWeek*, November 27, 2006.

18. IBM Press Room, "Majority of Global CEOs Plan Fundamental Change and Expect New Forms of Innovation to Drive Growth, According to IBM Study," March 1, 2006, www-03.ibm.com/press/us/en/pressrelease/19289.wss (accessed March 3, 2007).

19. Wendy Kopp, President and Founder, Teach for America, in discussion with the author, February 28, 2007.

20. See Collins and Porras, *Built to Last*, 94.

21. Ibid., 223.

22. Hamm and Symonds, "Mistakes Made on the Road to Innovation."

23. Michelle Peluso, President and CEO, Travelocity, in discussion with the author, January 4, 2006.

24. Steven K. Scott, *The Richest Man Who Ever Lived* (Colorado Springs, CO: Water Brook Press, 2006), 31.

25. "Tear Down This Wall," Ronald Reagan's remarks at the Brandenburg Gate, West Berlin, Germany, June 12, 1987, www .reaganfoundation.org/reagan/speeches/wall.asp (accessed March 3, 2007).

26. Antonio Villaraigosa, Inaugural Address, July 1, 2005, www.lacity.org/mayor/maysp1a.htm (accessed March 3, 2007).

27. Office of the Governor of the State of California, Arnold Schwarzenegger's Remarks at Tsinghua University, November 16, 2005, http://gov.ca.gov/index.php?/print-version/speech/1263/ (accessed March 3, 2007).

28. Obama 2010, Inc., Barack Obama 2004 DNC Keynote Address, July 27, 2004, www.obama2010.us/media/ (accessed March 3, 2007).

29. Cordell M. Parvin, "Law Firm Leadership," Cordell Parvin-Articles, www.cordellparvin.com/html_articles/parvin_law_ firm_leadership.html (accessed March 3, 2007).

30. Kim Wright Wiley, "Get Real! How Mark Burnett Sold Reality TV to America," *Selling Power* (May 2006).

31. Ibid.

32. Donald Trump, introduction, in Mark Burnett, *Jump In! Even if You Don't Know How to Swim* (New York: Ballantine Books, 2006), xi.

33. Michael V. Copeland and Michael Mortiz, "How to Pitch a VC," *Business 2.0*, December 1, 2004.

Chapter 3 Sell the Benefit

1. "I'm a Mac and I'm a PC," ad titled "Meant for Work," www.apple.com/getamac (accessed March 11, 2007).

2. "Why You'll Love a Mac" link on Apple's Web site, www.apple.com/getamac/stuff.html (accessed March 11, 2007).

3. Mike McCue, CEO and Cofounder, Tellme, in discussion with the author, December 12, 2006.

4. Definition of Intel's Dual-Core Xeon Processor from Intel's Web site, www.intel.com/products/processor/xeon (accessed March 11, 2007).

5. Intel ad from Web site, "With Intel® Built In, Bumrungrad Has Expansion Built In," www.intel.com/business/enterprise/emea/eng/builtin/bumrungrad/index.htm (accessed March 28, 2007).

6. Intel Web site link to view stories regarding "the human network," www.cisco.com/web/thehumannetwork (accessed March 28, 2007).

7. Guy Kawasaki, *The Art of the Start* (New York: PORTFOLIO, 2004), 46.

8. Wikipedia contributors, "Flash Memory," *Wikipedia, The Free Encyclopedia*, http://en.wikipedia.org/w/index.php?title=Flash_memory&oldid=135032579 (accessed March 11, 2007).

9. Eli Harari, Founder, Chairman, and CEO, SanDisk, personal communication with author, 2006.

10. Beverly Keel, "Meet Tim Russert," *American Profile*, January 15, 2006, www.americanprofile.com/article/5124.html (accessed March 11, 2007).

11. May Wong, "Data Storage Gets Image Makeover as Vegas Hosts Gadget Show Next Week," Associated Press Newswires, January 5, 2007.

12. Harry Beckwith and Christine Clifford Beckwith, *You, Inc.: The Art of Selling Yourself* (New York: Warner Business Book, 2007), 109–110.

Chapter 4   Paint a Picture

1. Myra Goodman with Linda Holland and Pamela McKinstry, *Food to Live By* (New York: Workman Publishing Company, Inc.), ix.

2. *Harvard Management Communication Letter*, a newsletter from Harvard Business School Publishing: The Manager's Guide to Effective Presentations: "Presentations and the Greeks: How Their Insights Can Improve Your Speaking Today" (1999): 11.

3. *An Inconvenient Truth*, DVD, directed by Davis Guggengeim (Hollywood, CA: Paramount Pictures, 2006).

4. "Presentations and the Greeks," 11.

5. Ibid., 12.

6. Kevin Crust, "An Inconvenient Truth: Al Gore Warms Up to a Very Hot Topic," Movie Review, *Los Angeles Times*, May 24, 2006.

7. Nancy Duarte, Principal, Duarte Design, in discussion with the author, March 9, 2007.

8. Cliff Atkinson, Author, *Beyond Bullet Points: Using Microsoft PowerPoint to Create Presentations that Inform, Motivate and Inspire*, in discussion with the author, December 8, 2006.

9. Ibid.

10. Cliff Atkinson, *Beyond Bullet Points* (Redmond, WA: Microsoft Press, 2005), xiii.

11. Atkinson discussion with the author.

12. Simon Cooper, President and COO, The Ritz-Carlton Hotel Company, in discussion with the author, December 8, 2006.

13. "Wow" story provided by public relations director for The Ritz-Carlton, San Francisco, e-mail message to author, January 30, 2007.

14. Howard Gardner in collaboration with Emma Laskin, *Leading Minds: An Anatomy of Leadership* (New York: Basic Books, 1995), 43.

15. Bono, "Because We Can, We Must," Commencement address for the University of Pennsylvania, May 17, 2004, www.upenn

.edu/almanac/between/2004/commence-b.html (accessed March 18, 2007).

16. Gerald Zaltman, *How Customers Think* (Watertown, MA: Harvard Business School Press, 2003), 37.

17. Brad Paisley, "The World," song, *Time Well Wasted* CD, Arista label, 2005.

18. Joel Osteen sermon, "Bringing Out the Best in People," #282, first aired on April 2, 2006, property of Joel Osteen, Lakewood Church, Houston, TX.

Chapter 5   Invite Participation

1. "100 Best Companies to Work For 2007," *Fortune*, http://money.cnn.com/magazines/fortune/bestcompanies/2007/full_list/ (accessed March 17, 2007).

2. Bill Powanda, VP, Griffin Hospital, in discussion with the author, January 9, 2007.

3. "Derby Hospital Executive Wins Deane Avery Award," *New London Day*, May 29, 2002.

4. Powanda, in discussion with the author.

5. Simon Cooper, President and COO, The Ritz-Carlton Hotel Company, in discussion with the author, December 8, 2006.

6. Steve Bates, "Getting Engaged," *HR Magazine* 49, no. 2 (February 2004), www.shrm.org/hrmagazine/articles/0204/0204covstory.asp (accessed March 18, 2007).

7. The Hudson Employment Index, "Hudson Survey Finds Gen Y Wants More Feedback, Access to Managers and Social Interaction than Older Workers," New York, October 18, 2006, www.hudson-index.com/node.asp?SID=7473 (accessed March 18, 2007).

8. Jay Adelson, CEO, Digg, in discussion with the author, October 18, 2006.

9. Marissa Mayer, Vice President, Search Products & User Experience, Google, in discussion with the author, September 21, 2006.

10. Pat Croce, *Lead or Get off the Pot!* (New York: Fireside, 2005), 121.

11. John Maxwell and Jim Dornan, *Becoming a Person of Influence* (Nashville, TN: Thomas Nelson, Inc., 1997), 85.

12. "Find the Other Person's Comfort Zone, Advises Talk Host King," *San Jose Mercury* (San Jose, CA), January 9, 2005.

Chapter 6   Reinforce an Optimistic Outlook

1. Del Jones, "Optimism Puts Rose-Colored Tint in Glasses of Top Execs," *USA Today*, December 15, 2005.

2. Marcus Buckingham, *The One Thing You Need to Know* (New York: Free Press, 2005), 66.

3. Michelle Peluso, President and CEO, Travelocity, in discussion with the author, January 4, 2006.

4. Celia Sandys and Jonathan Littman, *We Shall Not Fall: The Inspiring Leadership of Winston Churchill* (New York: PORTFOLIO, 2004), 173.

5. Ibid., 174.

6. Ibid., 179–180.

7. Mark Burnett, *Jump In!* (New York: Ballantine Books, 2005), 121.

8. Colin Powell quote, http://en.thinkexist.com/search/search Quotation.asp?search=Optimism+is+a+%27force+multiplier%27 (accessed March 17, 2007).

9. Laurence Gonzales, "The Biology of Attraction," *Men's Health* (September 2005).

10. Tiger Woods, *How I Play Golf* (New York: Time Warner Trade Publishing, 2001), 269.

11. Bob Rotella, "How to Drain Them Like Jack," *Golf Digest* (June 2001).

12. Robert J. Sternberg and Cynthia A. Berg, *Intellectual Development* (New York: Cambridge University Press, 1992), 332.

13. Oprah Winfrey quote, http://en.thinkexist.com/quotation/surround_yourself_with_only_people_who_are_going/323088.html (accessed March 17, 2007).

14. Anthony Robbins, *Awaken the Giant Within* (New York: Summit Books, 1991), 273.

15. Doug Ducey, CEO and Chairman, Cold Stone Creamery, in discussion with the author, January 25, 2007.

16. Bob Levinson, VP, Corporate Development, Lynn University, Boca Raton, FL, in discussion with the author, February 4, 2007.

17. Ronald Reagan letter announcing his Alzheimer's disease, November 5, 1994, www.reagan.utexas.edu/archives/reference/alzheimerletter.html (accessed March 27, 2007).

18. Colin Powell interview on CNN, first aired June 11, 2004, property of CNN.

19. Lisa Gschwandtner, "Mission Critical: Leadership Lessons from Colin Powell," Selling Power (September 2005).

20. Francine Knowles, "Oprah's Amazing Life," *Chicago Sun-Times*, September 29, 2006.

21. Gschwandtner, "Mission Critical."

22. Ibid.

Chapter 7   Encourage People to Reach Their Potential

1. Joel Osteen, *Your Best Life Now: 7 Steps to Living at Your Full Potential* (New York: Warner Faith, 2004), 133.

2. Richard Carlson, "Well-Deserved Compliments Boost Morale," Pioneer Press, section 7E, October 5, 2005.

3. "The Freaky Side of Business," *Training*, February 1, 2006.

4. Jim Thompson, Executive Director, Positive Coaching Alliance, in discussion with the author, February 7, 2007.

5. Sharda Prashad, "2 Business Giants' Secrets of Success; Creativity Not Enough, Eisner Says Branson Relies on Happy Employees," *Toronto Star*, September 14, 2006.

6. Mark Mastrov, Founder and Chairman, 24 hour Fitness USA Inc., in discussion with the author, January 31, 2007.

7. Ron Clark, Cofounder, the Ron Clark Academy, and Disney's American Teacher of the Year 2000, in discussion with the author, January 26, 2007.

8. Michelle Peluso, President and CEO, Travelocity, in discussion with the author, January 4, 2006.

9. Steve Jobs, "Stay Hungry, Stay Foolish," Remarks at the Stanford University Commencement, June 12, 2005, http://news-service.stanford.edu/news/2005/june15/grad-061505.html (accessed March 17, 2007).

10. Garth Brooks, "It's Your Song," song, *Double Live* CD (disc 1), Capitol label, 1998.

Chapter 8   HOO-YAH! Optimism Rules aboard the USS *Reagan*

1. Robert Labrenz, Information Systems Technician, U.S. Navy, email correspondence with author, February 17–18, 2007.

Chapter 9   Fifteen Minutes to Five-Star Service

1. Jason Rhodes, Assistant Director of Housekeeping and Laundry, The Ritz-Carlton, San Francisco, in discussion with the author, January 30, 2007.

Chapter 10   How a Visit to the Lower Ninth Ward Inspired a Nation of Givers

1. Peter Fleischer, Partner/Senior Counselor, Ketchum, in discussion with the author, January 22, 2007.

Chapter 11   Wow 'Em like Steve Jobs

1. Steve Jobs, Macworld San Francisco 2007 Keynote Address, Web site link title: "Watch the Keynote," www.apple.com/iphone/ (accessed March 27, 2007).

Chapter 12   How an Ice Cream Shop Became the Hottest Franchise in Town

1. Doug Ducey, CEO and Chairman, Cold Stone Creamery, in discussion with the author, January 25, 2007.

Chapter 13   A Mission Impossible Fit for Tom Cruise

1. Matt McCauley, Chairman and CEO, Gymboree Corporation, in discussion with the author, February 28, 2007.

Chapter 14   A Master Class in Motivation

1. Ron Clark, Cofounder, the Ron Clark Academy, and Disney's American Teacher of the Year 2000, in discussion with the author, January 26, 2007.

2. Tamara Lauriano, "In a Class by Himself," *Reader's Digest* (August 2006).

3. Ron Clark, *The Essential 55: An Award-Winning Educators Rules for Discovering the Successful Student in Every Child* (New York: Hyperion, 2003), 142.

4. Ibid., 158.

Conclusion   Be a Spellbinder

1. Robert T. Kiyosaki, *Rich Dad, Poor Dad* (New York: Warner Business Books, 1997), 141.

2. From *The Apprentice*, Season 6, episode replayed on CNBC, March 12, 2007, property of NBC.

3. Natasha Bedingfield, "Unwritten," song, *Unwritten*, Sony/Bmg Import label, November 23, 2004.

Index

About the Author

Carmine Gallo is a communications coach for the world's most admired brands. His clients have included Intel, Barclays, Nokia, Chase, The Home Depot, Dreyer's, Hyundai, L'Oréal, Clorox, SanDisk, IBM, Gymboree, and many others. Gallo is an Emmy Award–winning journalist who has worked as a business correspondent for CNN as well as anchor, host, and reporter for Fox, TechTV, CNET and CBS. Gallo writes a popular biweekly column on communications skills for Businessweek.com. He is also a media-training and presentation skills specialist for clients of Ketchum, a global public relations firm. Gallo's first book, *10 Simple Secrets of the World's Greatest Business Communicators*, has been translated into a dozen languages. His popular multimedia keynote speeches are a hit around the world.

Gallo graduated from UCLA and received a master's degree from the Medill School of Journalism at Northwestern. He lives in Pleasanton, California, with his wife and two daughters.

Visit the author at www.carminegallo.com.